HINDU HORSEMAN

HINDU HORSEMAN

LT. COL. DENZIL HOLDER

I thank my daughter, Sally, for the endless trouble she has taken, and the enthusiasm she has shown in getting this book into print.

D.H.

To our friends, and they were many.

First published by Picton Publishing (Chippenham) Ltd 1986
ISBN 0 948251 18 2

Printed in Great Britain by
Picton Print
Citadel Works, Bath Road, Chippenham, Wilts
PP52850

CONTENTS

LIST OF ILLUSTRATIONS

LIST OF MAPS

The Late Field Marshal Sir Claude Auchinleck
GCB, GCIE, CSI, DSO, OBE, LLD

FOREWORD

by
The Late

Field Marshal Sir Claude Auchinleck,
GCB, GCIE, CSI, DSO, CBE.

This is the story of an Officer of that famous regiment Skinner's Horse - one of the twenty-one regiments of cavalry of the British Indian army serving Britain after the 1914-18 war. I have known the author, Denzil Holder, from the days when he was a junior captain until he was retired because of the wounds he received in the Abyssinian campaign. Over the years he became a fine horseman, polo player and, by repute, an exemplary Squadron commander. He recalls his successes in the horse world, his visits to America and Central Europe while on leave, service on the North West Frontier of India, and the beauty of Kashmir. One can sense throughout his love for regimental soldiering, his care for the men and horses under his command and the day to day life of an Indian Army officer between the wars.

C. AUCHINLECK F.M.

INTRODUCTION

The title, "Hindu Horse", was a soubriquet applied to the Indian Cavalry by their British Cavalry counterparts.

* * *

References to 'India', it must be remembered, now comprise both Mohammedan Pakistan and Hindu India.

* * *

I write from memories stretching back for over fifty years. The book may contain some inaccuracies - and those better versed in the times can pick holes in it - but it is a Cavalry soldier's view of India as I saw it and I present it as a saga of what is now history, the British Raj, and our small part of it.

* * *

PREFACE

The year 1650 finds one John Holder, a Quaker and the seventh descendant of earlier known members of the family, in Barbados. There, for the next six generations, the family possessed at least eight big plantations and various smaller ones; they were very wealthy and had many servants and slaves to work their plantations. They built and owned ships to carry their sugar to Europe. They constructed fine mansions and, visiting England from time to time, had acquired houses in Grosvenor and Berkeley Squares, and estates in the country.

William Holder (b. 1721) is described as "A Dorsetshire Gent". His son William Thorp, educated at Eton and Trinity College, Oxford, was Sheriff of Dorset. The family then took to soldiering as did many sons of the gentry, and his son, John Hooper, was a Colonel (regiment not stated); while his son, my grandfather, Charles William (1822) started life as a Cornet in the 5th Dragoon Guards. He later bought himself the Colonelcy in the Scots (Fusilier) Guards which must have cost him a pretty penny - vide Lord Cardigan, who paid out 'over £40,000' for the command of the 11th Hussars, and commanded the Light Brigade at Balaclava. My father, Arthur Charles, was born at 33 Berkeley Square. I asked the compiler of our family tree what had happened to the family money and he replied, "I think it went mainly on expensive cavalry regiments and riotous living".

Charles William commanded the Brigade of Guards when they were training in Aldershot, driving over there in a trap from his house, Yateley Hall. He sent my father to Eton and the 12th (now 9th/12th Royal) Lancers, from which he retired on his marriage four years later. After passing out of Sandhurst he went on a world tour of India, Japan and America. As one reads the doings of officers in H.M. Forces in those times, they seemed to take as a matter of course time off to hunt, to travel or to spend with their loves - at will. On joining, my father had an income of £2,000 a year; that was in 1888.

My mother, the daughter of a penniless officer in the 54th Foot, quite unaware of the value of money, proceeded to ruin him. His financial affairs were in chaos anyway; his investments in such things as Argentine Railways and, I heard, Harods, became worthless. No gentleman at the turn of the century ever mentioned the matter of money. My mother, a fine pianist with a beautiful voice, was a descendant of the Derbyshire Cokes, who were the older branch of the Cokes (now Leicester of Norfolk), one of the oldest families in England. She redecorated our house every few years and demanded six children (my father only wanted two) - which she achieved. With a rapidly declining income, many servants, a stable full of horses and schooling fees for six children, capital was sold out year after year to meet expenses until there was very little left. My father had a kind nature, adored his wife, and should of course have up-ended her and put a stop to this business. Unfortunately he did not, so no British Cavalry for me. It had to be Wellington and the Indian Army. This explains why I sought my fortune in India - Cavalry of course - but on a lesser plane.

* * *

GLOSSARY

Bania	Money lender
Baratz	Peach branch
Bearer	Personal servant
Bell-hop	Page boy
Bhisti	Water carrier
Bibi Khana	Woman's house
Burrel	Mountain goat
Cantonments	Military Areas
Charpoy	String bed
Chattis	Earthen water pots
Chupattis	Bread pancakes
Daffadar	Cavalry sergeant
Dewali	Hindu festival
Havildar	Infantry sergeant
Hazoor	Your Honour
Horse Tonga	Taxi carriage
Jheels	Lakes
Khitmagar	Table servant
Kitna?	How much?
Kurta	Long tunic
Lungi	Turban
Machan	Platform in tree
Mam-bap	Father and Mother
Mohd	Mussulman or Mohammedan
Markhor	Mountain goat
Mullah	Tribal religious leader
Munshi	Urdu teacher
Nullah	Ravine
Oorial	Out-size wild sheep
Ovis Amon	Large mountain sheep
Ovis Poli	Large mountain sheep
Risaldar	Senior Indian Officer (Cavalry)
R.T.O.	Railways Transport Officer
Sahib bolta	The Sahib says/orders
Shikara	Gondola-type canoe
Shikari	Ghillie/stalker
Sirkar	Authority/Government

Stables	Grooming time
Sowar	Cavalry trooper
Syce	Groom
Tamasha	A 'do'
Tats	Tiny hill ponies

* * *

Champion Company, R.M.C. Sandhurst, 1918.
(D.H., 7th from right)

CHAPTER I

S A N D H U R S T

It was at 7.30 am on the 24th of April, 1918, that eleven companies of Gentlemen Cadets were drawn up in line for the last parade of my last term at Sandhurst.

Then ....."Champion Company .. attention .. slope arms .. by the right Quick March" and we, 'H' Company, led by the band, marched to take up our newly won position on the right of the line. Were we proud? I will say we were, bursting with pride in ourselves as the champion Company of Sandhurst and the fact that we had won our position by defeating the other companies in drill, musketry, games and riding. Thirty out of each hundred-strong company had 'passed out' and became, that morning, Commissioned Officers. The 'Right of the Line' has always been a position of honour in the British Army, and I, as Senior Sergeant, (there was only one Under-Officer) had a particular source of pride since I was, on that parade, the right-hand man of the entire Royal Military College. As the sun dispersed the early morning mist it became apparent that there was no customary jerry perched on top of the flag pole and no drapes of W.C. paper hanging from window to window in the upper storey of the old building behind us. A quiet end of term.

Sandhurst was fun and I loved it. Not all fun for, as 'Juniors' during our first three months, we had drilled for three hours a day and had been bullied and abused by our Staff Sergeant, Bill Harley, whose scarlet face, ginger moustache and stamping feet terrified us. But what advice and epithets he hurled at us were always prefaced by 'Sir'. "Mr. Holder, Sir, will you hold your rifle straight, Sir". In our early days, and in civilian clothes before our uniforms arrived, we blushed for shame when picked on. Later, one took it as a matter of course; staff had to damn someone every minute or so. The drill instructors were magnificent snobs, as befitted members of the Brigade of Guards, and when H.R.H. Prince Henry joined 'H'

Royal Military College Sandhurst

Company in my last term, Bill Harley was not one to allow a passing Officer to be unaware of the fact that he had a Royal Prince in his drill squad.

"Mr. Prince Henry, Sir, swing your arms, Sir", "Mr. Prince Henry, Sir, ___" and poor Henry, pink in the face just had to take it. He collected minor punishments like the rest of us and more than once, as orderly sergeant I, for some infringement, drilled him up and down the company passages after evening mess.

Sandhurst at that time was not very democratic. The cadets, drawn almost exclusively from the Public Schools, supported a code of decency and unselfish behaviour, and he who offended that code found himself in trouble, and extremes of diversion from it led to an ink bath. When I was an Intermediate (second term) it was decided to punish a youth, who in fact had not been to a Public School and was thoroughly uppish and objectionable. The offender was required to run naked along the length of the main company passage and back again, while those whose rooms opened on to the passage armed themselves with a wet and knotted towel and chastised the victim as he ran for his life. He was then immersed in a bath full of ink. The following morning on company parade the inspecting officer completely failed to notice that one of our number was pitch black. He knew!

While the third term seniors gave pretty good stick to the juniors, it was nothing like so tough as at Woolwich, the establishment which trained gunners and sappers. There a senior could order a junior, "Double, damn you", and the youth in question had to run out of sight of his tormentor. Should this happen on the playing fields or on the parade ground, it was a considerable distance before the junior could find cover.

I joined the R.M.C. in January 1917, a very cold winter. Coming from warm homes we found the Old Buildings, constructed in Georgian times, bitterly cold. The wind tore down the long stone passages and, although there were small radiators in our single rooms, we were never warm. On our first morning we were roused at 6.30, and proceeded with our rifles to a lecture room which went by the name of a Hall of Study. There we were faced for the first time with the dreaded Staff Sergeant Harley. To end the hour's session he told us that we would stand to attention "Without a move, mind" for one minute, which he timed. We were cold, hungry, exhausted with concentrated zeal, and before the minute was up, five of the thirty in the squad had fainted. Staff pointed out that before we finished we would stand to attention on Battalion parades for thirty minutes, which in fact we often did, and I can only remember one man falling out. That was after a forbidden night out in London which he repeated. He was caught climbing in and sacked. While under close arrest I, with other sergeants, had to guard him, and I remember his pressing me to look at postcards of naked women, which in this case I was not interested in doing.

Our doings were of little interest. Interminable drills, an hour's P.T. in the evenings in the Gym, musketry, topography, lectures on Military Law, Administration, Tactics, Hygiene. But it was not all work. I captained the R.M.C. hockey team, kept a motorcycle (a deadly sin) for which I bought black market petrol from old Pritchell in his one-time livery yard just outside the grounds. I coxed the first boat that the R.M.C. ever put into the water, and finally, after various races that summer, we deadheated with a hefty New Zealand crew in an inter-services regatta at Marlow. The final was the third race that afternoon and we had cycled fifteen miles or so to the river - not a bad effort for teenagers of eighteen. We were hard and fit and we made little of it.

With the passing-out parade my time, after fifteen months at Sandhurst, finished. Perhaps my best memories are those of our Company Commander, Richard Howarth, a splendid soldier who had got a D.S.O. at the Gallipoli landings. After the war he became a beloved Housemaster at Stowe, and of my friends - great fellows, great friends, and one's parting with them is examplified by that lovely Harrow School song, which starts:

> "Five hundred faces and all so strange,
> Life in front of me, home behind
> I felt like a waif before the wind ..."

and ends:

> "Five hundred faces alive with glee,
> Trials are over and term is done

With all its glory and all its fun,
And boyhood's dream is the past for me!
Yet the time will come, tho' you scarce know why
When your eyes will fill at the thought of the hill
And the wild regrets of the last goodbye."

and so it was.

Many of my term were killed in France in the six months before the end of the war. The expectation of life for a subaltern in the trenches was, I believe, in the region of a month, and in the Royal Flying Corps two weeks. I had tried for the R.F.C. but the powers ruled that having trained a ground based officer, they required that he soldiered as such. My second choice was the Indian Cavalry, and this I got.

Troops in those days were not sent out to India in the 'hot weather', so those of us intended for the Indian Army were attached to training battalions in England until the time came for us to sail. By some error I was posted to France with a draft of those who had completed their training. We crossed the Channel from Southampton in a large convoy of transports and escort vessels. During the crossing I caught the prevalent 'flu' which was sweeping Europe, and from which many thousands died. I struggled on, feeling like death. When we arrived at Le Havre, there on the quay was a big contingent of American wounded en route to English hospitals. They were a magnificent lot, all of them 6ft or more in height, whereas our lot at the end of the war were the scrapings of medical categories. Some lacked a finger, others toes, some were asthmatic, all were tiny. I stand 5ft 7ins. but was taller than four-fifths of them. All came from Birmingham and were tough and stout-hearted to a degree. Towards the end of their training they were vaccinated and inoculated for T.A.B. on the same day. The next day on parade one poor lad fainted. It was very hot that summer and we went to remove his tunic. His T.A.B. arm was so swollen that we had to cut his sleeves to free him, but he had lined up to parade and do rifle drill with the rest of them.

As we marched our lads along the line of Americans, there were ribald remarks from the Yanks.

Were we on our way to school? If so, why the rifles? We blushed but stepped out bravely. Yanks! Had we not been in the War for years before they came in?

On arrival up the line I was grabbed by a doctor, spent a few days on my back, and was then recalled to England as our India embarkation orders had come in. I returned to the rest camp at Le Havre, but sailings were held up as there was a violent storm raging in the Channel. After hanging about for 36 hours, a party of about twenty officers returning on leave were warned to board a destroyer. We cast off at 10 pm. and proceeded up the harbour. It was still blowing very hard. Very romantic to me to be aboard a Royal Navy ship in wartime, with the various coloured buoys which marked our way up the harbour, and I went up on to the bridge to see it all. I wondered where the others were. Then we reached the open sea. I had crossed the Channel many times as a child, but this! The destroyer bucked like a mad thing as only a destroyer can. Within moments I was sick on the bridge, sick descending the steps to the deck, sick again on the deck ... murder! I suppose I was not all that well after the 'flu; anyway, I found my way to the Wardroom, and there were the others all stretched out along the seats lining the walls. They were old soldiers and knew the form. There was no room for a greenhorn, so I lay down on the floor, which stank of seawater and vomit, and used my hard-packed haversack as a pillow. What a trip - I thought I would die. Not for me small ships in H.M. Navy!

During my embarkation leave I was friendly with a dear little theatre girl in London. When I had to go home she promised to write to me, and I instructed her to address the letter to the Golf Club and not to my home. Unfortunately, the Club re-addressed the letter, and on entering the house I was met by my two sisters with quizzing eyes, holding a letter out and asking:

"And who is this from, pray?"

Fearful, I thought to gain time by turning it over and to my horror there were two impressions in scarlet lipstick and below them S.W.A.K. I will translate for the moderns: "Sealed With a Kiss". Whose face was red?

* * * * *

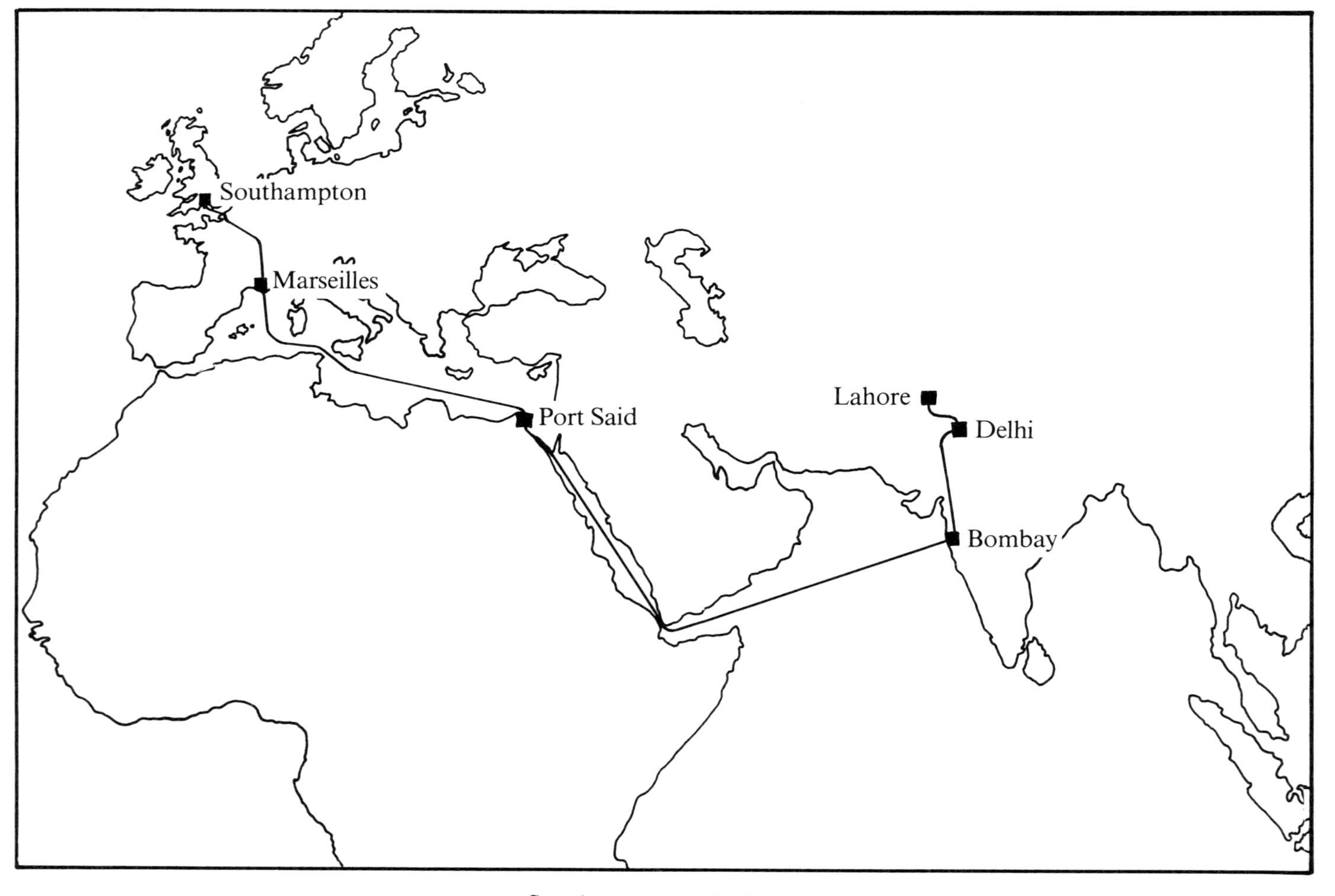
Southampton
Marseilles
Port Said
Lahore
Delhi
Bombay

CHAPTER II

TRAVELLING EAST

When I say 'we' sailed for India, 'we' refers to the Sandhurst contingent destined for the Indian Army.

Whether we crossed the Channel in convoy I cannot remember but we fetched up in, and were confined to, the Le Havre rest camp. A couple of days later we were moved to the railway station where the train was waiting to take us to Marseilles to continue our journey to India. Our train consisted of very third class carriages with wooden seats, no glass in the windows, no dining car and no lavatories - all very French - very war time. The train was immensely long and planned to take the hundred or so of us, and also the next intake into the war time cadet colleges of Quetta and Wellington, as well as the cargo for the ship in which we were to sail. On the platform, sergeants were bustling about, marshalling us to our carriages and issuing to each so many tins of biscuits, sausages, butter, tea etc. and a petrol-jelly cooker. When we politely enquired what this lot was in aid of we were told, "Rations, Sir". We, Commissioned Officers, were somewhat taken aback, but there in a heap were the goods, this was our carriage and the four of us had little time to get aboard before our three engines started to pull out. We somehow cooked our supper in the lid of a biscuit tin and did our best to sleep on the hard seats. Our journey to Marseilles occupied five days. After the first two, the carriage was filthy from cooking, spillages and litter and, being August, it was getting very hot. We relieved a porter of his station broom with which we cleansed the carriage and then climbed up on to the carriage roof which we cleared of soot and where, by day, we spent the rest of the journey. Wonderful scenery as we meandered slowly at fifteen miles an hour or so through central France. Then came the first tunnel. It caught us asleep during a hot afternoon when yells from up front alerted us that the shallow embrasure advancing upon us would surely sweep us off the roof to our death. We flattened ourselves and prayed like mad, but we need not have panicked as there was five feet of clearance between us and the roof of the tunnel.

There being no lavatory our only alternative was to walk along the foot boards to sit on the buffers at the rear of the carriage - an uncomfortable and risky enough seat at the best of times - but made moderately safe by clutching the rim of the buffer with one hand and the hand rail with the other. When the "need came" for another hand one's position became extremely precarious. Country-side halts often occurred alongside vineyards, where we nipped down and picked luscious bunches of grapes, which were more than welcome to augment our fare. At the stations, dozens of us made a bee-line for the lavatories and time and again some of our number, ensconced in the cabinets, were caught out when the train moved on, and were to be seen buttoning up their garments and racing up the platform to get aboard the train. The train increased speed - albeit slowly - but it was touch and go. When the platform ended they pelted along the rails, rapidly running out of steam and, cheered on by those aboard, either made it or were left behind.

We finally arrived, extremely grubby. We were housed in a delightful rest camp on a sea shore, and a week later embarked and set sail for Egypt. We were not torpedoed approaching Port Said - which was comforting - and arrived at a revolting rest camp at Kantara, half way down the Suez canal. A day or two later we entrained at midnight, heading for Suez. This time our conveyances were open trucks which were apparently lined with sand, into which we snuggled down, only to find at daybreak that the sand was coal dust. You can imagine our appearance in our previously immaculate new 'drill' (hot weather) uniforms. The rest camp was tented, dirty and dusty, and the mess tent black with flies. The food was filthy as were the Gyppy servants. On our second night there and in the hope of a decent meal, four of us went into Port Tewfik to the only, and ramshackle, hotel. We ate soup and, half-way through the fish course, I felt awful.

Dizzily I fled to the lavatory where I broke into a muck sweat. The sweat poured off my nose and chin as from a tap. Some minutes later I felt more like myself again, but my clothes were wringing wet. I had been poisoned but mercifully had sweated it out. On the last leg of our journey we sailed in a P & O steamer down the Red Sea and across the Indian Ocean to Bombay. This is one of the hottest voyages in the world and it was held that whichever way the ship was travelling there was invariably a following wind, which resulted in no breeze.

I saw a wonderful sight in the Red Sea. Too hot to sleep, I went up on deck at dawn. We were following a ship about one mile ahead of us, and just ahead of it, from the Arabian to the African coast, was a thick belt of birds in flight, some fifty yards in depth. It extended as far as the eye could see, just above sea level, but what species of birds I did not know. As the ship in front arrived at the line of flight the birds rose some 200 feet above it and descended again to sea level. By the time we arrived there were only a few stragglers left.

Bombay. I got up at 4 am and watched, entranced, as we closed in through numerous lighted beacons towards the harbour. The dawn spread and lit up the shore and white palaces on Malabar Hill and the docks. India. We had arrived.

The previous night we had, as often before, played vingt-et-un. We decided on a last hand before bed and a stake limit which was agreed at £5 each. I was the dealer and drew a 'natural' - an unbeatable ace and court card. My three opponents had good cards and doubled. I re-doubled, turned up my cards, and won £30 but needless to say never got paid. £30 was a subaltern's pay for a month!!

To celebrate our arrival we went to the Taj Mahal - the best hotel in Bombay and, thinking ourselves *'Sahibs'* at last and very dashing cavaliers, made our way to the cocktail bar and proceeded to order through the cocktail list from A to Z. I cannot remember how far we got but I know that none of us appeared at dinner that night.

Next day we went out and were amazed at the differences of dress and faces which thronged the streets. What were they all? We did not find out. In fact, apart from the cosmopolitan collection to be found in any port, Bombay has three main communities, Indian, Parsee and British. There are bearded Sikh taxi drivers from the Punjab, Pathan house guards from the frontier, and thousands of cotton mill hands. Add to this that every separate caste of Indian wore a different type of garb and you can imagine our perplexity. The streets were packed with traffic; trams, motor buses, taxis, bullock carts, bicycles and sundry cattle that roamed about unattended. There was little or no 'Rule of the Road' and confusion reigned.

'Embarkation' had informed me that I was posted to the depot of Sam Browne's Cavalry at Jhelum in the Punjab - some 1000 miles north of Bombay. I duly reported to the R.T.O. and boarded the Frontier Mail that went up to Peshawar in the North West Frontier Province.

On active service, or if you travelled east of Port Said, an important item of your luggage was a bedding roll and a '*chilumpchi*' - a tin basin with a leather cover in which you kept your shaving and washing gear. The bedding roll consisted of a made-up bed of blankets, sheets and a pillow rolled up in a canvas cover with straps to hold it together. Being a greenhorn I did not realise that Indian trains had no sleeping cars, so I had packed various treasures in my bedding, consigning it to the guards van. On entering my carriage I was confronted with two long bunks and two more above them and beyond the entry door space a bathroom with a basin and lavatory seat. The train pulled out at 4 pm and, alone in my carriage and reclining on my bunk without my bedding, I watched entranced as we puffed through the outskirts of Bombay and into the country beyond, with its crops of sugar cane and palm trees interspersed with jungle. As the sun went down smoke rose from the fires in the villages. Quaintly clothed brown people still worked in the fields, and bullock carts moved slowly along dusty tracks. This was real India.

We pulled into a station where the first class passengers alighted to dine in the station restaurant - a five course meal. As I returned to my carriage I realised that it was considerably cooler than Bombay and during the night it was positively chilly. This was nothing to the following night between Delhi and Lahore, when in early October it was extremely cold.

On arrival at Jhelum I was met by Travers Calder, a cordial war time officer from Jamaica, with the regimental brake, drawn by a four-horse team. He told me that the depot was camped some four miles out in the country, owing to an outbreak of cholera in cantonments.

Indian Cavalry
by Snaffles

After eight weeks travel I had at last arrived - at a regimental depot it was true, since the regiment was still on service in Mesopotamia, but I was at last with the Indian Cavalry.

* * * * *

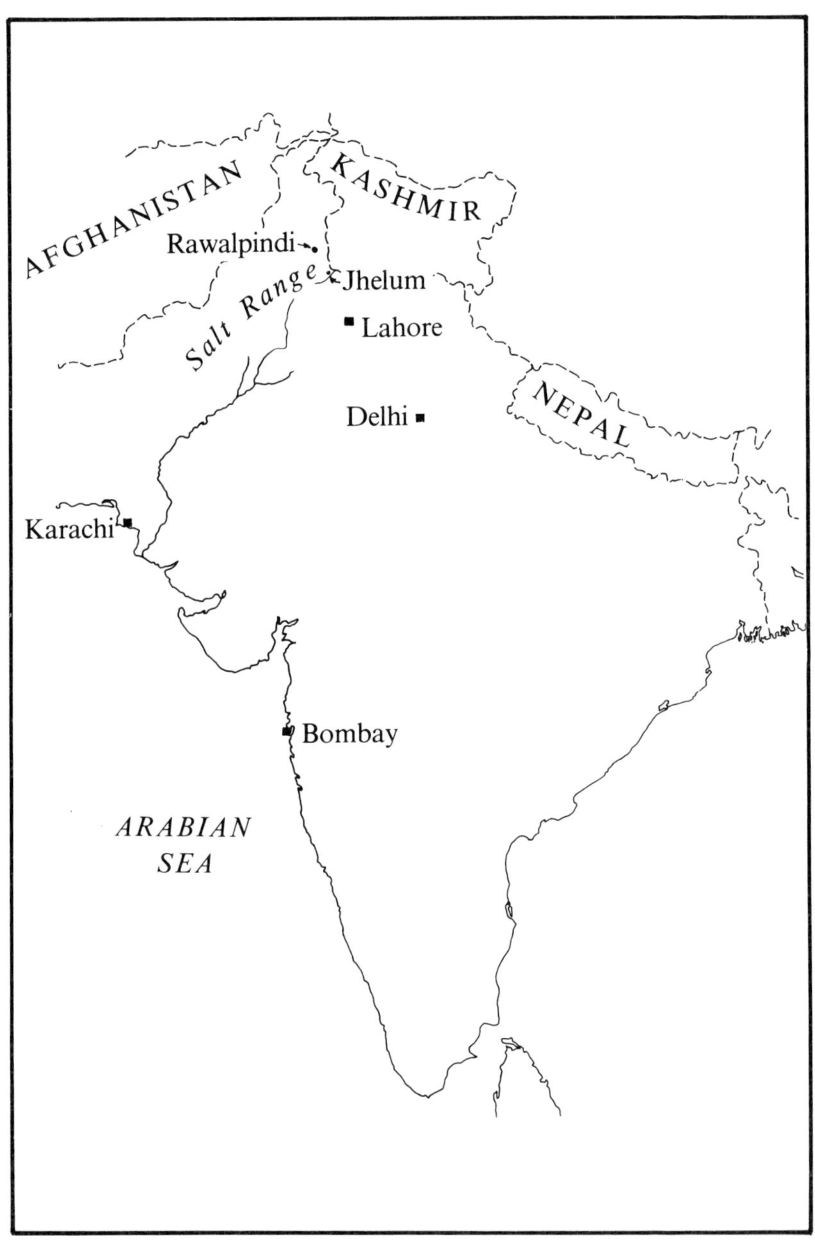

Jhelum: North West India

CHAPTER III

JHELUM (1918 - 1919)

Jhelum was a delightful little station situated on the banks of the Jhelum river which flows down from Kashmir 200 miles to the north and with the three other rivers of the Punjab, joins up with the mighty Indus. It had a considerable timber trade from pine trees felled in the high forests of Kashmir and floated down the river to be collected and processed in the saw mills of the city. The Grand Trunk Road, from Calcutta to the North West Frontier, ran between the city and the cantonments, and crossed the river over a mile-long bridge carrying a railway line alongside the roadway.

The cantonment normally held an Infantry Brigade in peace time but, during the war, it housed two Cavalry and eight Infantry Depots, which were training establishments to supply reinforcements to units fighting overseas.

Jhelum had many good points as a station. It provided a magnificent view of the snow-crowned range of the Himalayas 80 miles to the north. The river still retained the chill from the snows, and this kept the air reasonably cool during the fierce heat of the hot weather. There was a considerable variety of sport to be had, the foremost of which was polo, and there I learned the game which was to be my abiding interest throughout my service. Added to this there was excellent shooting ... wildfowl near the river with partridge and *oorial* on the Salt Range hills.

At Tangrote, some four miles upstream, was to be found the mighty *mahseer*, a species of carp caught on an enormous spoon attached to a hawser-like line. The first rush of the *mahseer* far outspeeded that of the salmon. Jhelum was situated halfway between the polo and racing centres of Lahore and Rawalpindi. What more could a young officer ask of life?

On arrival, I was introduced to the Indian officers, large, courteous gentlemen, who put me in the way of my duties.

These were not onerous, chiefly that of riding around the many recruit riding schools, each marked out by small mud pylons on the parade ground.

The War was practically over and soldiering was not taken all that seriously. I found it difficult to employ my Sandhurst zeal because I could not speak the language and, in those days, very few of the Indian officers (I.O.s) spoke English. I trained up a hockey side that beat most of the Infantry Depot sides whose game it was, just as ours was polo. Playing both games three days a week and often shooting at the weekend, I took a prodigious amount of exercise, and ate to match it. It seems inconceivable now, the amount that one did eat. A four-course breakfast - fish, meat, eggs and bacon and lashings of toast and marmalade, topped up with fruit. Then a four-course lunch and a five-course dinner. I was nineteen, still growing and needed every mouthful of it.

Every station in India had its Club, a meeting place at the end of the day where the 'civilians' - legal, police, forest and canal officials, and the soldiers met, and which provided the polo grounds, tennis courts, billiards, bridge, a bar and a 'snake pit' - a derogatory term for what today would be called 'the Lounge', and where the ladies foregathered and gossiped and were offered drinks by their admirers. I must declare that in those days I was 'right-minded': I had no ideas other than to save enough money to buy polo ponies, saddlery, guns, smart clothes and the like, and also to pass my three Urdu (Indian language) exams which each officer posted to an Indian Unit had to pass or be reverted to British Service. So I did not go to the Club, but after the evening game or exercise, sat down with my *munshi* (Urdu instructor) and swatted away at the language until it was time to change for 'mess'.

The language was not all that difficult but the text books and written exam papers were written from right to left in Persian characters, which were a bane to me. As a child I was quite good on the piano - I played by ear but could never make much of the lines and dots of the music score. Later, I had a go at learning German and was again faced with their ghastly script. I haven't got a photographic eye and, amongst other things, I have never been able to spell for the same reason. My *munshi* cost me a rupee a lesson, which was a jolly sight cheaper than drinking at the Club, and anyway I did not drink.

I was mad keen to shoot an *oorial* - a species of large sheep with tremendous horns, which were to be found in the Salt Range hills. Often on Saturdays I would leave cantonments with my orderly and a pack-horse and, after a twenty mile ride, fetch up at a shepherd's hut where we spent the night. Tired out, I would see the horses watered and fed, partake of a simple meal of *chupatties* and curry provided by the shepherd, and stretch out on the hut owner's *'charpoy'*. The hut would have a small fire of aromatic sticks and dung, and around it the shepherd, my orderly and a few adjacent hillmen would congregate, smoke a hookah and no doubt discuss the sahib; behind them a few goats would huddle. How pungent the smell of the fire, how fierce the stink of the goats, how romantic the glint of the flames in the goat's eyes; and I slept.

At 6 am my orderly would waken me with a cup of tea heated in the embers of the last night's fire, and I pulled on some clothes and accompanied the shepherd out into the bitter cold of the coming dawn to seek out an *oorial* grazing peacefully at that early hour. I wore a khaki cotton shirt and trousers and a pullover, which I would discard later on when the sun came up and which served as an elbow rest when taking aim over a rock or sharp stone. One's usual shot was anything from 200 to 400 yards. To start with, I used an Army 303 rifle, but later on bought a .280 Ross rifle which had a flat trajectory up to 500 yards and therefore did not need to have the sights reset for different distances. The Salt Range hills were volcanic, lying in ridges some 300 to 400 yards apart. As I topped one ridge I hoped to see some *oorial* on the face of the next ridge. If I shot one, the shepherd would run like a deer and cut the animal's throat before it died. The Mohammedans were only allowed by their religion to eat meat thus butchered; the idea being that the flow of blood cleansed the carcass.

On a subsequent visit with a party of others, my *shikari* stalked me within 50 yards of a magnificent head. The ammunition that I had bought with the Ross rifle was four years old, and I had four mis-fires; at each click of the bolt the herd moved away and finally disappeared over a cliff as I fired my last shot. Too late, the ram had gone. A few weeks later, the same *shikari* was instrumental in getting this same animal shot. I think it was 34 or 36 ins in length, nearly a record. What was important to me was the crystal clear air, the wonderful vista of the plains below, and the exhilaration of one's youth. Thrilling too were the pug marks of a panther and her cub that circled the rest-house in which we lodged one night. Various enthusiasts went after her, but she always evaded them.

In the winter the crops, except for sugar cane, were gathered in, and one could ride out in any direction with no obstacle to one's passage except for the next river, which might be a 100 miles away. Apart from the horse sports of polo and pig-sticking, I loved riding - the warm air and the perfect going underfoot. And very romantic it was returning in the evening through the little mud villages in the centre of which stood the village well which was a vast affair, and from which the wives and village maidens drew their supply of water and carried it home in earthenware *chattis* on their heads. I was 20. There were no English girls in India just after the war and one cast a very interested eye on these shapely young women. Above was the line of snow capped mountains clothed in a glorious pink from the rays of the setting sun. I would shake my mount into a trot to get home before dark so as not to stumble in the rutted track.

On arrival, there was the pony's groom waiting for us and my bearer (personal servant) shouting for the *bhisti* (water carrier) to bring the bath water that he had heated over a fire and which he tipped into a tin tub. Light in the bathroom was provided by a hurricane lamp and, in the bed-sitter, by an Edwardian oil lamp with its globe shade. Electricity was ten years away and we lived with few frills.

Shortly after I joined the depot, its Commander, Guy Hutton, arrived in my squadron lines during 'stables' and said that he would look me out a charger. None of the officers at that time owned their own horses and so rode one of "King George's" out of their squadron. Hutton had an exceptional eye for a horse and later became the chief purchasing officer in Calcutta, where the Remount officers bought annually some 2000 animals imported by the shippers from Australia to supplement those bred in the Army Remount horse farms, and which mounted both the British and the Indian cavalry regiments. Puffing his bulldog pipe, Hutton stopped behind a grey gelding, asked a question or two from the troop leader, and said, "There you are". He turned out to be a good ride with a nice disposition and did me very well. One afternoon, I was riding him across country and we arrived at a seasonally dried out river bed. It was known as the 'Tiger Nullah'. I had heard of its reputation for treacherous quick sands but did not know where they were. I started to ride across its 200 yards breadth when the horse stopped and snorted. I looked and there were footmarks of cattle about, so I pushed him reluctantly on, and in a few strides he sank up to his belly, a moment later up to the saddle flaps. I nipped off and went in up to my waist. I thought, "This is it". The horse was terrified, screaming and plunging, but somehow he got a foothold and, rearing up, threw himself backwards and was on solid ground. Luckily I had kept hold of the reins and by the grace of God he heaved me out too. In the struggle the bridle came away and I was left holding it as he galloped away. I was also left with a fear-stricken heart - another moment and we would have both disappeared below the surface of the river bed. Some villagers caught the animal and I rode him home in a very chastened frame of mind.

Of all the many religious festivals, there was one, Dewali, which was very charming. The myth had it that on that night the god Krishna passed over the houses and if he saw a light he would bestow a blessing on the household. So, each householder placed a light - actually a wick in oil in a tiny crucible - on the roof of his dwelling. Such a light only cost a farthing, which could be afforded by the poorest, so the great majority lined their roofs and doorways with these lights spaced about a foot apart. I was taken into the city by an Indian Police Officer serving for the duration of the war, and I was enchanted by the sight of the rows of tiny pinpoints of light shining in the bright still air, outlining each house. Later, when I was married, we gave a few rupees to the servants who decorated our bungalow likewise, and each pony's stall had its personal lamp. Dewali took place in October and symbolised to us the start of the 'cold weather' - India's winter - something we had waited for for six months.

The following year a Punjabi Regiment subaltern, Rainsbarth, bought a ticket in the Calcutta Sweep on the Derby and drew, if not the favourite, one of the fancied horses. The winner of the sweep drew an enormous sum of money. A body known as the Greek Syndicate always offered to buy the ticket on the fancied runners at odds slightly less than the current odds. Rainsbarth waited all agog for the arrival of their telegram, which it did indeed at the telegraph office. But the telegraph clerk, reading their vast offer, went round to the timber merchants, who were the richest men in the city, and who, after conferring, made Rainsbarth an offer which was only a fraction of that offered by the syndicate, and which he refused. The clerk then delivered the telegram, but before Rainsbarth could accept it the race had been run, his horse was disqualified and poor Rainsbarth only collected Rs.2,000 for having drawn a runner. Such is fate, although it must be said that Rs.2,000 was a princely sum in those days to a subaltern.

Prior to the war, each Indian Army entrant had to spend a year with a British regiment who reported on his suitability to join the Indian Army and, during this time, the entrant had to pass exams in Urdu (the language of the army - men being recruited from all over India and talking some thirty different languages). So a language 'of the camp' was established, common to all and taught in the regimental schools. I sat for the first of these, an oral exam, before a board of somewhat disinterested officers headed by my depot commander Guy Hutton, who had only one idea in life - that of breeding and racing horses. All of a tremble I was horrified when Hutton told me to translate "The animals went in two by two, the elephant and the kangaroo". Such stuff was completely outside the syllabus that I had sweated through so assiduously with my *munshi*: '*Hathi*' was an elephant but what in God's name was a kangaroo? There weren't any in India. I flustered through this and a few more questions, and sweating with apprehension, was relieved to hear that I had passed. Anyway Hutton was far too kindhearted to fail his favourite subaltern.

Talking about my *munshi*, a good looking young Pathan, which name covers the various frontier tribesmen, we discussed all sorts of things during our evening sessions and one day he steered the conversation round to women. Would I like to have an Indian girl? (Would I not!) The outcome was that I and a friend met him one night at the entrance to the native city and followed him to a house where two little females were produced. Mine led me up rickety stairs to a small room containing a hurricane lamp, a chest and a string bed. She closed the door and my heart hammered madly. She was a sweet little affair with her wheaten skin and huge dark eyes, and, as very modestly she slipped off her sari, I looked on her small half-lemon breasts and her dark blue silken hair. She was little more than a child.

We returned to the Cavalry lines, satisfied after all those months and not really ashamed, though such behaviour was not 'in' for the sahibs of that era. Fifty years before the Europeans had all kept native girls, and very sensibly too. The practice of co-habiting with native women had its merits, not the least of which was that the young officers, with their "sleeping dictionary", learned to speak the language idiomatically, which we never achieved. We talked what was known as 'sahib's Urdu', but this was well understood by the troops many of whom had also had to learn this language. Our mess was very old and still had its '*Bibi khana*' (womans' house) in the compound, its windows barred, and this was where the girl-friends had lived. With the arrival of the white wives this practice was largely discontinued!

As there were a very few officers in the depot, I was in command of a squadron - but it was really administered by the senior Indian Officer who, because of his age, had not gone on active service with the regiment. My Risaldar, Sant Singh, was a wonderful character, a Sikh in his sixties, six foot and broad to match, his beard (all the men in those days were bearded, as were our own previous generation) was going grey. While we were attending 'stables' (the grooming of the squadron's 100 or so horses) he would take upon himself to put me wise as to the duties and circumstances that pertained to a junior British Officer. I knew when this was coming as, prior to his discourse, Sant Singh would adjust his spectacles, and then say ... "Now Sahib, we will talk about money". I was to save up for my two months' 'hot weather leave', also for my eight months' leave home, which usuallly came about every third or fourth year. I was to have nothing to do with horse racing, never to borrow or lend money, and not to marry until I was a Major Sahib. He would illustrate his advice with examples of British Officers that he had known in his long service.

"My X Sahib married as a captain and he had nothing but trouble".

"My Y Sahib waited until he was a Major Sahib, always plenty of money, and he was a very happy sahib",

- and so on. Did I follow his advice? Well, in fact as it happened, I did, though it was not all of my choosing. Dear old Risaldar Sant Singh - my heart warms to him to this day, after fifty years.

In those days the men were able, with the permission of their squadron commander, to take their horses on their annual two months' leave. Their animal was inspected prior to departure and on return. One wretched youth had a grey - really a completely white horse - and during his leave there was a wedding in his village. Weddings, as all the world over, were a big '*tamasha*' in the life of the village and this lad was prevailed upon to lend his animal for the use of the bridegroom. The groom's family then proceeded to paint the horse with an array of highly coloured blotches, yellow, green, red, etc., which paint the owner was told would wash off - but in fact the various dyes were unremovable. On return to the depot the appearance of the animal caused something of a furore and the owner received a rocket and a punishment under some paragraph of the Indian Army Act, which covered every possible delinquency from murder to theft or rape. If no particular section of the Act applied there was always "Committing an act prejudicial to good order and military discipline". You couldn't win. A chap at Sandhurst was nailed under this section for farting in the R.M.C. chapel. The staff sergeant attending the parade ran him in - I know because I was the cadet sergeant on duty in the company orderly room next morning.

About six months after I joined I was warned to sit as a member of a Court Martial. The court consisted of a major, a captain of about four years' service and Holder. The charge was that of "Desertion in the face of the enemy" - the army's most heinous crime for which the maximum penalty was death.

The evidence showed that the accused, a simple country youth who had just passed in the ranks from his recruit stage, had been warned for a draft from his depot to join his regiment in Mesopotamia. The day before the draft was due to entrain, this boy received a letter from his widowed mother telling him that the (one) cow was ill and he was to come to attend to it. What to do? The troop train en route to Karachi stopped at a station a few miles from his village and the obvious thing was to stop off, attend to the cow and take a following train to rejoin his party. Of course when he arrived back to the station he had no separate ticket. He was apprehended and returned to his Depot under arrest.

Had he absconded from the troop train en route to service? He had. Guilty of charge? Guilty. The President of the court turned to me, the junior member and said,

"Lieutenant Holder, what is your sentence?"

There was I, dressed in my best tunic, breeches, boots and sword, invited to condemn the poor fellow to death. My heart was in my mouth, I broke into a sweat - for I had joined the army to soldier and to play polo, not to condemn my fellow creatures to death.

Through dry lips I stammered,

"Death, Sir".

I had no option. I was doing my duty as I, all too well (Sandhurst trained) knew it. The President turned to the captain,

"Your sentence?"

Reply, "Transportation for life, Sir".

The President drew on his pipe (the Court had been cleared for sentence) and said, "I think that six months imprisonment will suffice".

Gradually my heart-beat returned to normal.

* *

In those days, as in England prior to 1914, the horse was the main means of transport, and so everyone wore riding kit, usually jodhpurs; during the war one even dined in jodhpurs. There was only one motorcar in the station, a model-T Ford, belonging to the Judge, a highly paid civilian. The rest of us, when we could afford it, bought a trap and harnessed a troop horse to go in the shafts. I remember feeling very proud when I bought mine, a two-wheeler which went under the name of a 'Tum-tum' and cost about £10. I had my photo taken in it and sent it to my father, who was then serving on the Western Front, having joined up for the duration.

I had been just a year in the Depot when I was selected to attend the next course at the Cavalry School. It was really a course for captains and I was very young to go, so I was much envied and very proud to be chosen. Students at the course were required to take two chargers (parade horses). Sant Singh advised me to take a bay mare out of my squadron, and there was another excellent little brown gelding that had won a point-to-point which I should have taken, but in 'A' squadron was a Jemadar (one star) who was a wonderful little horseman and show-off. He had a brown gelding which he had taught all manner of tricks; he would stand in his saddle and tent peg off him. Like an ass I was glamourised into taking this animal. He was leggy and unsound and within a month of my arrival at Saugor he went, and remained, lame and was returned to the Depot. Still, I had done some very successful horse coping and departed to the Course with four quite useful polo ponies which I could just afford to keep. I did not drink and hardly smoked, though cigarettes were then only 7 pence for 50.

I have very happy memories of Jhelum, my first station. The glorious climate of the Punjab winter, my polo at which I was getting quite proficient, our Indian soldiers and my friends. Although of a happy nature, looking back, I don't think that I had a very happy teenage - my father was at the war, my mother inconsequent, and our reduced circumstances. Here in India I was out of it all and on a brand new wicket. Life was in front of me.

* * * * *

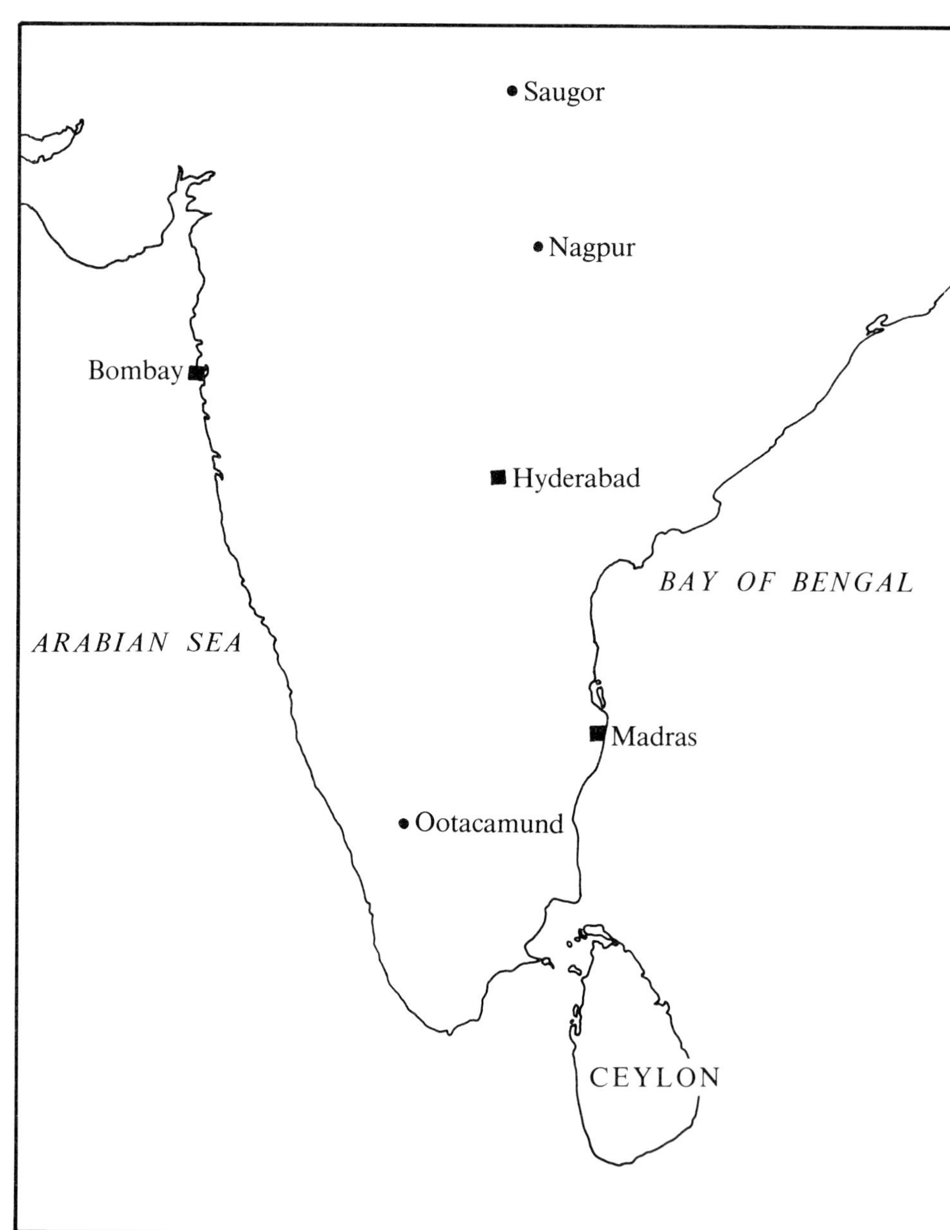

Saugor: Central India

CHAPTER IV

THE CAVALRY SCHOOL

All young cavaliers, if they were lucky, attended the eight month equitation course at the Cavalry School; Saugor, in Central India, or at Weedon in England. The course embraced both officers and N.C.O.s of both British and Indian service regiments, and one met and worked with representatives of some 40 regiments. Our instructors were picked horsemen who had earned a 'D' (Distinguished Report) on a previous course. We officers were divided into four rides, each with a ride instructor, under a Chief Instructor-in-Charge. Mindful of the honour of representing one's regiment at this, the first post-war course, I enjoined my orderly to keep my two chargers and four polo ponies in top condition and my bearer to turn me out impeccably.

That night I studied the mess kit of my companions. Cavalry mess kits were skin-tight overalls over wellington patent-leather boots, with double yellow lancer stripes down the seams. Skinner's Horse, which I was to join later, wore a yellow jacket. Other regiments wore scarlet, dark or pale blue or buff jackets with varying coloured waistcoats. We presented a very striking assembly. On parade we wore khaki - cloth in winter and cotton drill in summer. But there were differences in cap badges, shoulder chains and Sam Browne belts and their clasps; all very important to young officers.

We paraded for three hours daily, one hour on our chargers, another with our second year (half trained) remounts and a third competing with our first year remounts - a wild, initially unbacked animal from Indian Cavalry horse farms, or from the outback ranges of Australia, which took six weeks of long-reining and soothing before one was allowed to try and mount them. Time after time these horses could be seen galloping crazily back to their horse lines, trailing long reins, having broken away from their handlers. Later in the morning we attended lectures - tactics, topography, military law and the intricacies of administration. In the afternoon we played polo, did sword drill or hacked - if our bottoms were not too sore. I made some grand friends at Saugor. I was, bar one, the youngest in the course but being already fairly proficient at polo was accepted by various of my betters - dashing captains of three or four years' service. We all pretended we had lots of women and drank immoderately. In fact, our experience with women was minimal and we drank very sparingly as we could not, keeping up our horse establishment, afford to do otherwise.

Sword Drill, Saugor

Mounted parades were exciting or a slog, depending on the mood of our ride instructor. They must have been pretty boring for him - round and round the riding schools, all these in the open and gradually digesting and practising the art of 'High School' equitation. As our 'seats' and 'hands' improved we made occasional dashes over the jump courses or the steeplechase jumps on the race course and perilous adventures down the railed-in jumping lanes,

"Cross your stirrups",

"Fold your arms, Prinsep, Mostyn-Owen, Holder".

We legged our mounts to the first obstacle and breathed a short prayer.

During the course every student had to give a twenty minute lecture. I was a modest youth and the prospect of standing up on the lecture dais before my seniors appalled me. Furthermore what was I to lecture on? I had no active service experience and knew practically nothing about anything. I scanned various copies of 'The Cavalry Journal' in the hope of an idea and happened on an article on "Silladar Cavalry". This would do - it had to! I tore it out. The fateful day arrived.

"Holder, let us hear from you."

I staggered up to the rostrum clutching my article in a sweaty hand. I dared not look up at the assembly below. My voice shook but somehow I got through the ordeal. There was the usual mild applause - I should jolly well think so, seeing that the article was written by an eminent soldier! As I crept back to my seat I passed the desk of the senior instructor, Major Skinner, who beckoned me,

"Very nice, Holder", and in a muted whisper, "Cavalry Journal 1918 wasn't it?" It was.

Shortly after we arrived we had to write an 'operation order' dealing with a tactical situation which had been explained to us. I had never studied the military manual which dealt with the operation of war, and had not the faintest idea how to set about it. An operation order consists of stereotyped paragraphs, each dealing with an aspect of the operation in view, which in this case involved a night march. I put down a lot of tripe about bandaging bits lest their jingle gave our progress away and a few other inspired gems and handed it in. When I got it back Skinner had written in red ink,

"Dear Holder, - this reads like a novel."

I had much to learn.

In February, 1920, came the Cavalry School Point-to-Point races and, to do well in them helped one's end of Course report. I entered my little bay mare (my charger) in the lightweight race. She was an amenable ride and in spite of lacking any sort of breeding she had a reasonable chance if she lasted 2½ miles. I was somewhat apprehensive as the fences were stiff and we had never tackled jumps at racing speed. The fourth fence out was one with a wide ditch on the landing side. I was lying second to David Prinsep by a couple of lengths. He cleared the obstacle but, on landing, kicked back a cloud of dust which obscured the ditch to my mare, who dropped her forelegs into it and we took an awful purler on to the rock hard surface. My topee saved my face above my mouth but the rest of it was torn to ribbons. The remainder of the field swept over us and when I gathered my wits and sprang up to get remounted there was my poor little mare dead. She had broken her back. I wept - bitter tears of disappointment, and for the mare, who had done me so well for the past four months. As I walked back to the start John Gilpin (son of the famous trainer Peter Gilpin, and my best friend) came forward to comfort me. He put his arm round my shoulders, but I could say nothing to him. John was a grand fellow - the epitome of a Cavalry Officer. I was hauled into hospital, de-gritted and given an anti-tetanus injection.

The last excitement of the course was the Remount Chase on the race course, - for second year remounts. Each of the four rides was to put up two entries. Harold Flemming (King's Dragoon Guards), our ride instructor, selected Mostyn-Owen's big upstanding grey Australian and, much to my surprise, my short-legged stuffy little animal - also a 'waler'. I owned no racing silks but Harold Flemming came to my aid and very kindly lent me his racing colours - yellow with a blue hoop - the same as the Skinner's Horse polo vest. Flemming put me up in the paddock and, as I went out, patted me on the knee with the re-assuring words,

"Safe home!"

We lined up and the starter gave us the 'off'. None of these remounts had ever tackled jumps except at a collected canter - but now they had to gallop. The pace was all too slow and after a couple of furlongs I said to "Mossy" alongside me,

"Come on, let's quicken it a bit"

and the two of us went on. At the final turn I was leading but realised that at any moment Mossy's big grey could walk past us. I cleared the biggest jump on the course - my little brown mare jumping splendidly - when there was an almight crump and Mossy had come down. Two jumps, a furlong out and the winning post was in sight but my mount was tiring fast. Behind me I could hear fast approaching hoof beats and there was Atty

Persse on a lively little country-bred coming up on us fast. He arrived at our quarters at the final fence and then blew up, and we staggered past the post for a 'B' ride win. Harold Flemming was a very elegant horseman and had better manners on a horse than anyone I have ever known.

One of the highlights of the course was the 'Hundred Mile Ride' when we rode our chargers on a cross-country course off the map, to be completed in twenty-four hours. In place of our usual polo saddles was a parade saddle, a big clumping affair with attached Ds on which was hung one's sword, a feed bag of grain, a picketing peg and head rope, and a saddle bag stuffed with rations - the lot known as 'marching order'. We started off in pairs one morning after breakfast, each pair receiving their route. The pace to be averaged was 7 m.p.h. for fifteen hours including stops.

During the late afternoon it became apparent that we must do better than our walk and trot, especially if we were to get any sleep that night, so we urged our unwilling animals into long canters. Come midnight the four of us were flaked out and we unsaddled and dossed down for three hours or so. It was not all that cold but a saddle makes a hard pillow. Anyway we were too tired to worry.

We eventually arrived back at the school with time in hand - which was the important thing. Had either of us cast a shoe we would have had to walk in dismounted. The rest of the day was a holiday - and did my bottom need it! I sank on to my bed until time for mess. There we foregathered and many were the tales of excitements and troubles en route. All of us had lost our way at one time or another, one pair had woken in the night to find a panther stalking their horses, another had been entertained by a forest woodman whose offer of his wife had been gratefully accepted - or so they said. Two chaps reported that their partner's horse had gone dead lame and had to be fetched in, and so on. Quite an experience and the going had been shocking in places - rock and bog, rivers to cross and jungle to penetrate.

There was plenty of sport to be had. Polo on Mondays, Wednesdays and Fridays, pig sticking and fishing in various rivers, with big game in the jungles which abound in Central India. Two or three fellows would rent a 'block' of jungle for a month and proceed there for week-ends or for our Christmas or Easter breaks. A *Shikari* (stalker) would be engaged, and if there was a tiger or panther in the block he would arrange drives and beaters, or tie up a goat and put up a *machan* from which to shoot. The quarry would usually arrive at dusk or soon after to kill its night's meal. With, say, twenty beaters, at a shilling a day, the method of beating was beyond the means of the subalterns and 'sitting up' was the accepted practice. Even this involved a series of goats or calves to keep the big cat in play until the hunter could get out at week-ends. All this was beyond my pocket, so we youngsters ranged through the jungle on foot hoping to meet up with a quarry - which was usually a buck of the various species found in Central India. I shot a few of these beautiful animals but my heart was not in it. I had no killer or collector's zeal and felt a mean wretch when I looked at its dead body and its glazed eyes - the most poignant aspect of death. I did some *shikar* that year but was never tempted to return to the jungles thereafter, though keen *shikaris* took a block for their two months' leave regularly throughout their service. Even if I had been a keen shot, there was another objection to big game shooting: the best time of year to find the game was in the hot weather, when they congregated near such water as had not dried up, and I hated the heat of the summer.

During our Christmas break I had a thrilling experience. I had gone out early in the morning in the hope of getting a young peacock for supper. I had had no success and by nine o'clock I was tired and sat down to rest in the bright sunshine. Shortly afterwards I heard monkeys chattering and the whistling of *chital* (spotted deer), a sure sign that there was a tiger or panther in the vicinity. I walked towards a gap in a line of cactus in front of me and there, thirty yards away, was a magnificent tiger, his tail curved over his back and purring gently to himself. I had a .22 rifle - only suitable for very small game but I thought:

"What if Holder bagged a tiger with this diminutive weapon. If I shot him in the eye, would I not kill him?"

Sense prevailed; I had been taught never to go for 'cats' without a large bore double-barrelled rifle, as often there was no time to reload a magazine rifle when the quarry charged, and many had met their death by not observing this rule. The tiger walked on and disappeared into a *nullah*.

People at home seemed to think that India was populated by Rajahs, elephants, tigers and snakes. Later, in high places, I met various Rajahs and their ceremonial elephants, but this was the one tiger I saw at close quarters during my twenty-eight years in India.

Practising River Crossings, Saugor

On our last evening but one we had a celebration "guest night". We had a lot of unaccustomed drink, and a succession of extremely rude mess songs. At 2 am our favourite instructor, Andrews, led a conga type dance which he informed us was "The Ballet of the Fairies". This he headed very daintily and, on its conclusion, he was uproariously acclaimed and promptly rolled up in one of the ante-room carpets. This was considered tremendous fun, but the carpet had not been beaten since the course started eight months previously and was permeated with dust. When the poor fellow was unrolled he was unconscious, nearly suffocated. We might easily have killed him.

We paraded the next morning, on our first year remounts, and with monumental hang-overs. As we were falling in, "Frog" Harris who was always in the forefront of any barney, arrived in full uniform but topped with a bowler hat. Screeching a 'view halloo' he set off at a gallop, promptly followed by all four rides - off the parade ground and away into the country beyond. Our carefully nurtured mounts, that had never been out of a very collected canter, really thought that life had returned to them at last. Pulling like trains and well out of hand, they covered many more miles than their riders ever meant them to. No more work that day. Our instructors smiled and forgave us.

The Cavalry School was a milestone in every cavalryman's service. Hard work, gay times and good friends. My horsemanship was enormously improved and my polo handicap raised from 0 to 2, having represented the school in two tournaments. I did not achieve a D - just a 'good' - 'a very good type of young officer'. My C.O. was satisfied. So was I.

At the end of the course we were due for our two months' hot weather leave, and I was intent on returning to Kashmir. But one of the company plugged the virtues of Ootacamund in the South India province of Madras. As most of the army soldiered in the north-west and Saugor was half-way down to the south, four of us, John Gilpin, Mossy Owen, Nipper Wakeham and I, elected to take our leave there. Ooty was the summer (hill) station of the Madras Government - some 6,000 feet high. We obtained quarters in the Club, which offered the usual tennis courts and a golf club. There was a pack of hounds that hunted jackals over the sweeping downs of the Nilgiri hills which descended steeply every so often down to a bog-lined stream, rather like Devon and Somerset country.

I was fortunate to be lent four hunters and, on my first day out, when reaching one of these declines I took a sharp pull to avoid breaking my neck. To my chagrin various young women swept past me. Their hunters had learnt the technique of placing their forelegs stiffly out in front of them as brakes, and skidded down propelled by short strides off their hocks. None of my animals were Ooty-trained but after a bit we got the hang of it.

Those old enough will remember that 1921 was in the era of the dancing craze. Everyone danced. Every town hall or garage that had previously been given over to roller skating now became a dance hall, and thus it was in the Ooty Club as well.

We four bachelors were in great demand, and we shamefully attended both tea and dinner dances, and duly fell in love with one or other of the girls that we met.

As was incumbent on every visitor to a seat of government, we left calling cards at Government House, entering our names, address and duration of stay in the visitors' book. In due course we were invited to a 'Government House Ball'. On arrival an A.D.C. ushered us into the ballroom which, like others of its type, was adorned with magnificent chandeliers and with full length portraits of past and present Sovereigns. At one end of the room was a low dais upon which stood two gilt thrones for His Excellency the Governor and his Lady. We had never seen such grandeur. Apart from a few soldiers in uniform the men were in tail coats - many of them sporting decorations, the women in their best dresses. I, for one, felt right out of it, such affairs having no place in little Jhelum, and I backed against a wall watching my betters waltzing and two-stepping around. Suddenly there appeared in front of me a magnificent apparition in white satin and diamonds. She held out her arms and I was invited to dance. This was none other than Her Excellency Lady Willingdon, wife of the Governor, Lord Willingdon, who was later Viceroy of India and later still Governor-General of Canada - an aristocrat if ever there was one. But why this? Marie Willingdon was a woman in a million. She rode to hounds with the best of them, managed the G.H. with a commanding touch, and was a splendid hostess. Her Excellency had spotted a very young and very shy subaltern guest, obviously right out of his element and had left her throne to entertain him. I put my arm round her ample figure and she danced me three times round the room. Typical of her great and generous nature. Her natural warmth and gaiety made her extremely popular with the Indian Princes who were, by nature, somewhat reticent and shy.

At the end of that leave and following the Cavalry School, I was down to my last £20 in my bank account. To my credit I was never once over-drawn - almost unheard of in the army - but I had seen my family's money slipping away all through my childhood and I was very money-conscious.

* * *

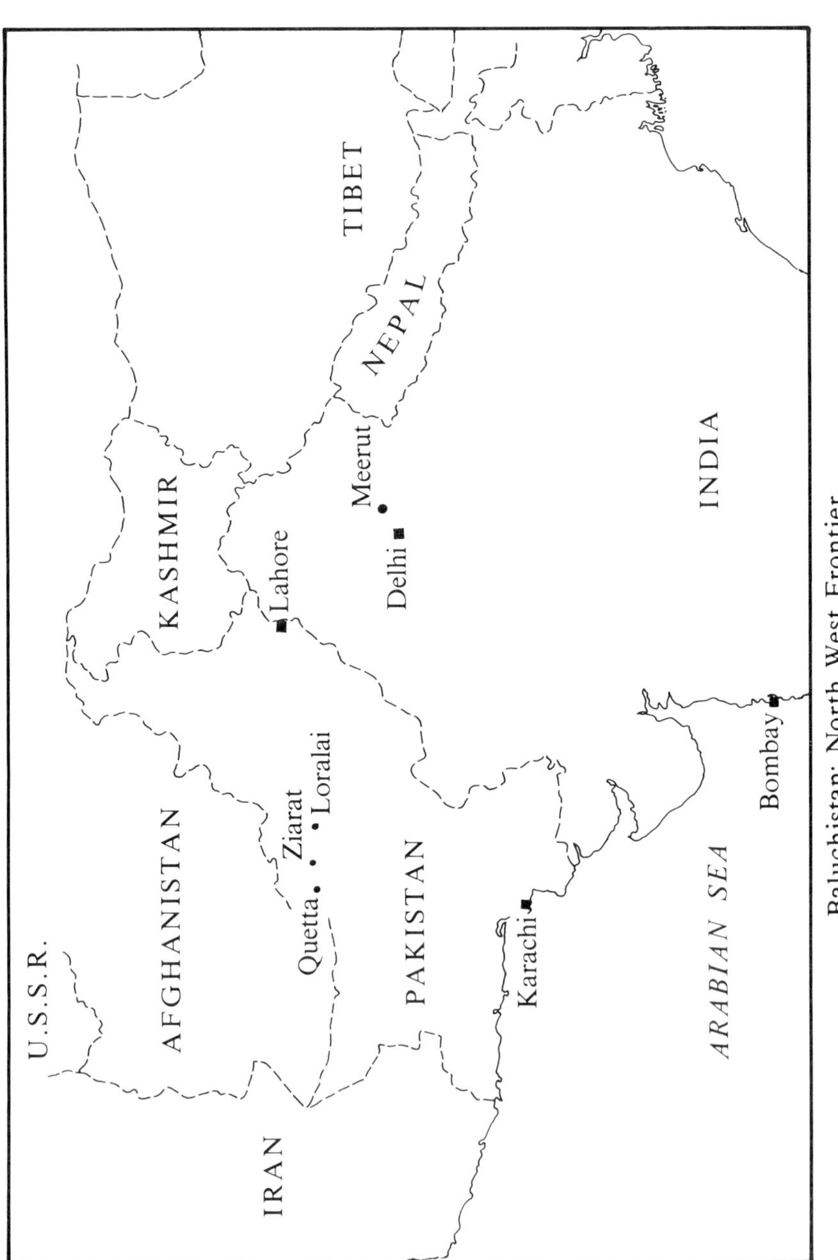

Baluchistan: North West Frontier

CHAPTER V

BALUCHISTAN

Since I had left the Depot in Jhelum the regiment had left Mesopotamia and moved to Loralai in Baluchistan in the far south-west corner of the frontier, and there I rejoined them. The North West Frontier was the scene of continual active service, where a considerable force of troops was stationed to counter the frontier tribes. These Mohammedan tribes, loosely called Pathans, inhabited the barren ranges between the Indus valley of India and Afghanistan. Their terrain produced the meanest of crops - their food, and scrub bushes which maintained their flocks of goats, and that was all. This area was administered by political officers, transferred from the army, who endeavoured to keep the tribesmen from misbehaving themselves in accordance with their treaties and subsidies which the Government of India doled out to each tribe. This worked pretty well as long as their wretched crops needed attention, or until some fanatical *mullah* preached sedition. Then the young men demanded a foray on the wealthy villages across the border, where a fat money-lender could be robbed or a girl abducted and held for ransom. When matters got out of hand the 'Politicals' ceased negotiating and advised the Government of India to send in a column - which could be a mixed brigade - to beat up the malcontents, blow up their watch towers (little forts) and inflict what loss they could. This often produced a battle royal when the locals opposed the advancing troops from positions of advantage on the hills bordering the line of advance, or secreted in *nullahs* en route.

Woe betide the soldier captured or wounded and left behind in those running fights. He was tortured and skinned alive or, at best, murdered and then mutilated. It was a point of honour, however hard pressed the troops might be, never to leave a comrade behind, but on occasions it did happen when on regrouping a man was found to be missing. These frontier wars were bloody affairs.

To combat the depredations of the tribesmen, a specialised form of tactics was evolved, known in the manuals as 'mountain warfare'. The column deployed parties in front of them (the advance guard) and picquets of platoon strength (30 men) to occupy the hill summits on the flanks of, and in advance of, the column in order to deny these vantage points to the enemy. As the column passed, each picquet descended and joined the rear. This was the danger moment. The tribesmen would lie low until a picquet packed up and left their position, when the opposition rushed to the summit and poured fire on the soldiers as they retired back down the slopes to the valley below. Only the Ghurkas, being themselves hill men, could compete on even terms with the Pathans during these retirements. Many were the casualties incurred during these picqueting operations and God help the coloumn that did not make camp before darkness fell.

The North West Frontier tribes could by large-scale operations have been smashed at any time, but there was an 'old school tie' outlook about the whole business. The N.W.F. Patrol was part of the way of life of the Indian army and provided first class battle training for the British and Indian regiments stationed there. All regiments in turn did their stint on the frontier.

Prior to the 1914 War there was a special corps entitled The Punjab Frontier Force, consisting of both cavalry and infantry, who were permanently stationed on the frontier, and who proudly affixed F.F. (Frontier Force) after their names and earned the nickname of 'Piffers'. Sam Brownes - the amalgamated 22nd and 25th Cavalry - was in fact a 'Piffer' regiment.

Loralai was a nice little station in spite of its complete isolation from India and from its nearest neighbour Quetta - some six hours motoring over a very indifferent stone road. It was situated some seventy miles from its railhead, Harnai, a station of the India-Quetta railway. The road from Harnai wound up steeply over a pass with innumerable hairpin bends for some twelve miles before it reached the elevated plateau known as the Zhob Valley. Quite regularly a posse of tribesmen raiders would sneak down from the heights and waylay an approaching car round a blind corner, shoot up the occupants and decamp with their belongings and, the big prize, their rifles issued for the journey. During my two years in the Zhob, a dozen or so British officers lost their lives on this stretch of road.

Some years before a Political Agent, while touring the district, put up for the night at one of the rest houses along the road. A section of Indian infantry had been sent down from Loralai to guard him. The *havildar* (sergeant) of the guard reported to the P.A. who told him to let his men have their evening meal before he posted the sentries. The *havildar* saluted and withdrew. The P.A. in question was a man of immense stature and strength and was known and feared throughout his district. His bearer unpacked his few tour belongings, laid on his bath, produced shaving water and went off to arrange the Sahib's supper. As the P.A. shaved he saw in his mirror the door of the room slowly open and a villainous face appear round it. The P.A. continued his shaving and watched the intending assassin with a twelve inch knife steal across the room towards him. As the knife was raised to strike him he whipped round, caught the knife arm and hurled the intruder across the room. He jumped on him to pin him down, shouting for the guard, but the assassin had a second knife in his belt and struck the P.A. in the stomach. The guard rushed in but all was over with the P.A. The guard commander had the murderer cut into small pieces and strewn about the rest house compound. Years later when I was trekking in the Himalayas, I chanced on a very old village headman, who discussing his soldiering days, told me that he had been the self-same commander of the guard.

The Zhob Valley had, in the time of the Moghuls, been a vast granary of corn; but owing to a change of climate it is now barren grit, sand and shale, except where water has been brought down from the hills by underground water channels into the Loralai cantonment. There everything flourished - crops and trees and, in the mess garden, grapes, nectarines, peaches and apricots for the picking. The station held only two regiments, ourselves and a battalion of the Bombay Grenadiers. The cavalry provided a troop in each of three forts along the road, ending at Fort Sandeman, which housed a further infantry battalion. A subaltern was detailed to command each of the forts for a fortnight at a time, and a pretty lonely and boring time it was. The troop - men and horses - were housed within these 'Beau Geste' forts from which sentries posted on the walls surveyed the surrounding countryside. The forts were positioned to cut off parties raiding into British India. On arrival at Loralai I was appointed station staff officer. I had an office in the shady mess garden and with the help of two Indian clerks administered the road, drains, bungalows, vagrants and the rest camp, where parties moving up and down the line put in for the night - the duties of a miniature urban district council. I was my own master and only supervised by the O.C. station - actually our 2nd-in-Command when he had a moment to spare from his regimental duties.

In a station where very little went on except normal regimental training, polo on a very indifferent ground with few players and some tennis, our only interest was that of augmenting our small monthly pay cheque with "travelling allowance" - known as "shaking the T.A. tree". It worked as follows. Travelling allowance was scaled at 11 annas a mile per person. Three of us would find excuses to visit one or other of the forts, and we then hired a battered old model-T Ford car at the cost of 14 annas a mile, which showed a profit of 6 annas a mile for each of us. On a round trip of 60 miles, this brought in each of us 22 rupees - the keep of a pony for a month.

On such trips we took our shot guns as well as our rifles, in the hope of a partridge which fed on camel dung along the road. The Fords had no windscreens. The driver shot forwards, and those in the back had a shot if the birds swung right or left. The occasional bird we bagged and the chance of being ambushed by raiders added spice to the journeys.

One evening, information was passed by our P.A. that the most wanted raider at that time - one Baz Khan - was to visit a woman at some caves about 25 miles up the road. It was arranged to send out three trucks to arrive there just before dawn. I was detailed to go with Charles Trehane in charge of the party. We set off at 4 am armed to the teeth and halted half a mile short of the four caves. We crept forward, stationing three men to cover each cave. It was my job to shine a torch into each cave which I did, with a pistol (.45) in the other hand. It was a bit dicey as I was outlined from inside against the brightening sky. I did not have my head blown off, as all the caves were luckily empty. Some months later a mounted patrol from one of the forts spotted a raiding party of three and gave chase. As they closed on the raiders one of them let fly with a rifle but missed, the patrol galloped in and killed all three with their swords. One of them was Baz Khan. There was a reward on his head and this was shared out among the lads of the section.

Christmas was approaching and we needed a Christmas tree for a children's party we were to give in the mess. So, combining business with pleasure, we motored up to Ziarat, some 30 miles on the Quetta road, where conifers were to be found, and mounted a *chikor* shoot. The *chikor* is a large version of the French partridge, whose habitat ranges from Spain, through the Balkans, Persia and Afghanistan to the frontier. A posse of locals was laid on by our P.A. as beaters. These hill-men, as agile as goats, scaled the precipitous rocky slopes and drove the game down various *nullahs* and over the guns stationed at the bottom. *Chikor* fly fast on the flat but with the height to help them were a hundred yards away one second and over one's head and gone the next. Wonderful sport in the brilliant sunshine and snow under foot. We also bagged a brace of hares - white in their winter coats. A tree was secured and we drove home happily in the piercing cold with good Christmas fare on board.

The tea was a triumph, our cooks surpassing themselves with meringues, jellies, sugar cakes and, the *piece de resistance*, three-tier Christmas cake full of raisins, nuts and all the choicest ingredients. Rather to our disappointment the children toyed with the small eats, each of them only having eyes for the famous cake. Large slices were cut and handed round but after a bite or two their portions remained uneaten. One of us tried a bit and "Oh God" - it stank of kerosene oil. The cook's mate had cut up nuts, or whatever, on a board on which kerosene had been spilt.

Our Colonel put on a stage show, a musical, in the mess anteroom, written and produced by himself, which was really first class. Two attractive girls had arrived for the winter and were roped into the play. Needless to say all the subalterns fell in love with one or the other of the girls, myself among them. My choice and I had a romance. We rode and danced together, and looked into each other's eyes as lovers will, and my one thought was marriage with this marvellous soul-mate, a life of loving bliss stretched endlessly before us. She, mercifully, was harder-headed than I and, on a certain occasion, I remember her whispering in my ear from the depths of my arms,

"Darling, you are pure gold but if we married I would be a millstone round your neck all your service."

Hard words when I was 22 but how true! True also the advice of dear old Sant Singh in Jhelum. I was plunged in misery for a year and a half. Much truth also in Maurice Chevalier's song in 'Gigi' - "I am glad I'm not young, any more!"

In February (1922) four of us subalterns went down to Meerut, 1,000 miles away in the Punjab, to play in the Subaltern's (polo) Tournament. Baluchistan, like the rest of the frontier, was bitterly cold in the winter and to protect ourselves from it we, like the natives, wore coats made from goat skins, the fur inside and with the outside skin of leather dyed a bright ochre, trimmed with gold embroidery, with astrakan fur round the seams and the collar - a very much finer garment than those worn by present-day 'hippies'. Having motored to the rail-head at Harnai, we boarded the overnight train to Lahore, where we had to change trains to Delhi and Meerut. Waiting on Lahore platform, sitting on our bedding rolls and clutching our rifles, we must have presented an unusual sight.

We were a good team, although we had had no fast polo or competition in Loralai, and won our way to the final where we met the 11th Hussars. An Indian cavalry team had never won the Subaltern's previously, always losing to the British cavalry who had over twice our strength of officers and could afford far better ponies than we could. In fact, we had no private ponies and all of us were mounted on troop horses. Further, while we became captains after four years' service, their subalterns soldiered on until a senior left the regiment and everyone below him stepped up in rank. We were out-gunned and out-ponied and lost by 5 goals to 2.

Meerut was a cavalry brigade station (3 regiments) with artillery and 3 or 4 infantry regiments and it was very gay during the inter-regimental week - this being by far the most important tournament played at the same time. Very different from quiet little Loralai. There were dances and parties every night for a gathering from all over India - an eye opener to us.

Back in Loralai things seemed very dull especially as the hot weather was due, when half the regiment would be on eight months' home leave or on two months' leave in the hills, and others were doing 'courses' - musketry, signalling, equitation and the like. We youngsters did not take our two months' leave since Baluchistan, being high, was not all that hot and we needed to save our money.

Loralai was a shocking station for malaria - the malaria mosquito breeding in countless numbers in our many irrigation channels. There I re-contracted the disease which hit me regularly every fortnight. I could feel it coming on - headache, burning eyes and pains in all my bones; within an hour I had a raging temperature of 105ö or so and poured with sweat. My bearer would change my pyjamas and bed linen which became wringing wet every two or three hours during the eight to ten hours of the attack. I would also shake to such an extent that I would ask one of my friends to sit on my shoulders to steady me up. When the fever had burnt itself out I was utterly drained and as weak as a kitten. The only remedy at that time was doses of quinine; this utterly foul stuff did not cure the illness but served to reduce the patient's temperature. Later, in the 1930's the medical services procured the American drugs that they had produced to clear malaria out of their settlements in Panama, and very efficient they were. Thereafter it was no longer a case of,

"Where is so-and-so?

"Oh, he had a bit of fever"

and this applied to our soldiers as well as British officers. Malaria is a beastly thing because the bug can stay hidden in one's insides and can emerge years later and after one has left malarial regions. I was lucky in that after leaving Baluchistan I got shot of it - this being possibly aided by the fact that I was promoted to Captain and allowed myself, with my extra pay, a peg of whisky each evening. This I am sure gave me the necessary boost to ward off further attacks. The thing is that darkness falls very suddenly in the east, with very little twilight. We exercised prodigiously during the day with 1½ hours mounted parade, an hour's walk round 'stables' and polo, hockey or tennis in the afternoon and at the end of the day we had taken a lot out of ourselves. Then the sudden dusk and gloom and we were at our lowest ebb before our evening meal, and that was the moment when the mosquito emerged to pierce our skins and inject its poison into our veins. A tot of whisky was the best palliative.

The year following amalgamation had little impact on us younger ones initially, but it soon became apparent that the majority of the (extra to normal) intake of 1914-1918 officers were to be drafted out, and many of our seniors as well. We, juniors, enjoyed our soldiering madly and most of us wanted to stay on serving, but orders proclaimed that three out of four had to go. I was lucky to be selected to stay on, but many of my friends departed.

Sam Browne's had a particularly good lot of subalterns and after the weeding out still had too many per the normal intake, so the senior, junior and middle seniority fellows stayed in the regiment and the remainder were put on the market to other C.O.s. Skinner's Horse applied for me and to them I went and there, for various reasons, I was very pleased to be. With them I spent the next 22 years of my service.

* * * * *

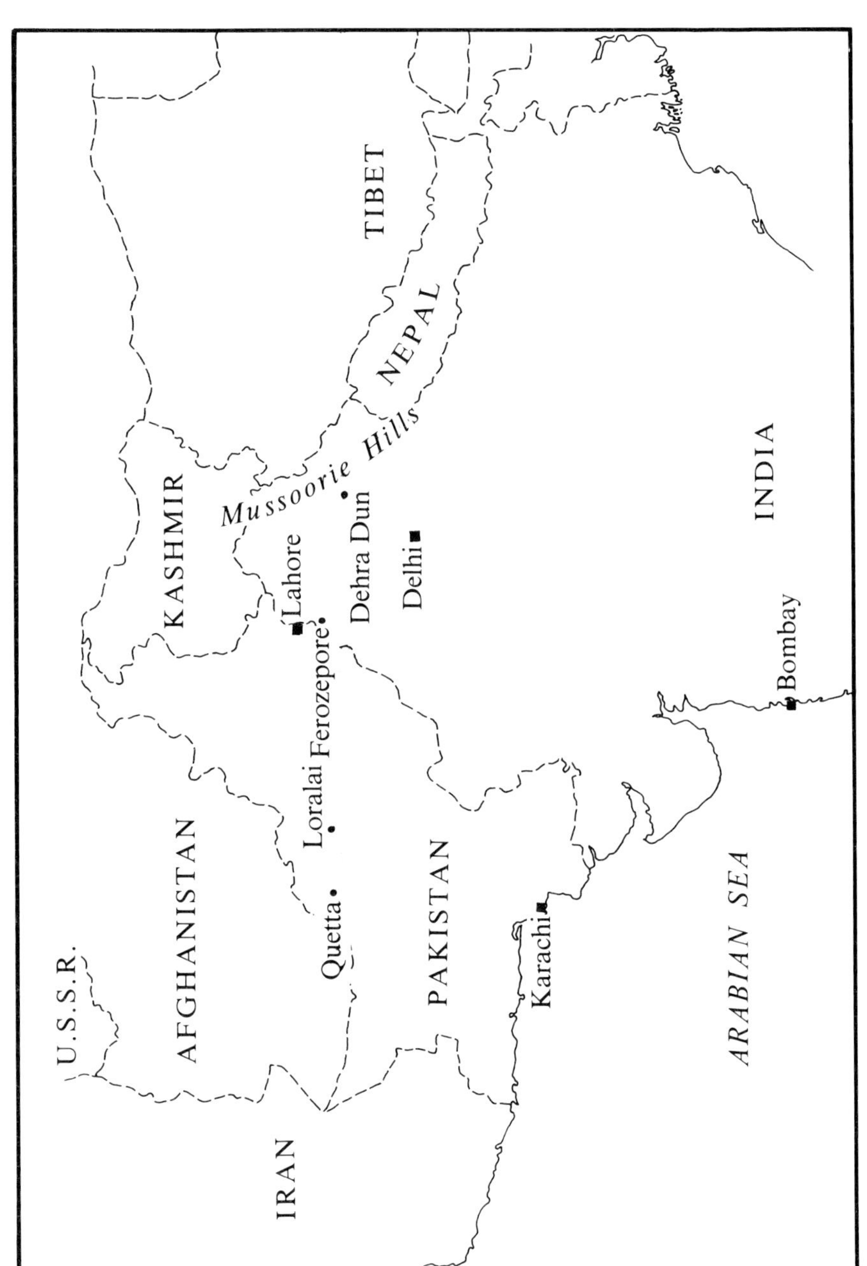

Ferozepore: North West India

CHAPTER VI

SKINNER'S HORSE - FEROZEPORE (1923-1927)

Skinner's Horse were stationed at Ferozepore, which lies between Lahore and Delhi, in the Punjab, and on the fringe of the Scinde desert, and for that reason very hot and dusty.

Up to 1918 there had been 39 regiments of cavalry, but after the war the army was reduced: the cavalry to 21 regiments, the majority by amalgamation. Skinner's Horse embraced the 1st and 3rd regiments raised by two brothers, James and Robert Skinner respectively, in 1803 and 1814. Both the full and the mess dress of the 1st was yellow - the only regiment in the army to wear that colour. The 3rd wore dark blue. After the 1914-18 war, full dress was discontinued on account of expense, but our mess dress carried on the tradition, and consisted of the yellow jacket with a black stand-up collar and cuffs edged with an inch of thick gold braid; as was the front and back of the jacket. Beneath this was a dark blue velvet waistcoat, high to the throat and frogged across the front with twists of gold cord. The assembled company looked splendid round the mess dinner table of dark, almost black, mahogany, loaded with the mess silver. In the 'hot weather' this mess dress was reproduced in white drill, and was worn with a yellow silk cummerband. The table was the Chillianwalla table on which, after the battle of that name, the corpses of eleven cavalry officers were laid out prior to burial.

In the early days of the take-over of India by the East India Company which, in the interest of trade and to quell unruly peoples on their borders, progressively annexed the countries of Bengal, Oudh, the Mahrattas, the Sikhs and Afganistan. Great battles were fought with considerable (oxen drawn) artillery on both sides, but the strength of each side lay in the staunchness of the Company's infantry and the hordes of native cavalry, the winning factor invariably being the leadership of the Company's British officers and the bravery of the British soldiers.

Colonel James Skinner, the founder of the Regiment, was the son of an officer in the Company's employ, and originated from Aberdeen. His mother was said to be a Rajput Princess from people famed for their honour and courage. James entered the service of the Mahratta Maharajah Scindia (who could muster 50,000 horse) and in whose employ, as a lieutenant, he commanded the equivalent of a brigade. The Mahratta high command were chary of promoting Europeans above the rank of captain, though Sutherland and three Frenchmen, de Boigne, Perron and Bourguoin, did in fact hold supreme command in Scindia's armies.

After various encounters, the British finally broke the power of the Mahrattas when Lord Lake with 4,500 troops defeated 19,000 under Perron at the battle of Delhi, the Frenchman having sacked all his British officers as 'unreliable'. Lord Lake offered service to the cast-offs, and Skinner was given command of 3,000 horse, who had also sought their pay from the British. This corps became the famous 'Yellow Boys' - Skinner's Horse. As part of the bargain, Skinner had requested, and been granted, assurance that he would never be called upon to fight against the all-conquering 'Company Bahadur' - the East India Company. At this period of war and counter-war, bribery and intrigue, it was not uncommon for commanders to change their allegiance, usually taking their troops with them. Since the days of chivalry, a victory would be celebrated by a banquet, to which captured generals would be invited and offered service with the victors. Soldiers of fortune had to earn their living with someone.

When it had been decided to "have a go" at, say, the Sikhs, the C-in-C ordered his forces to foregather at a certain rendezvous; the time chosen was that of the start of the cold weather - the campaigning season. A standing army is expensive to maintain, especially cavalry, and the E.I. Company with an eye to their shareholders' profits, evolved a system whereby irregular regiments, usually cavalry, were virtually employed for a particular campaign. The C-in-C would negotiate with commanders such as Skinner,

"How much to provide 1,000 sabres for ... months?"

A bargain would be struck and then Skinner would summon his proposed squadron commanders and agree to so many rupees per month for a mounted trooper. These (big men in their districts) then contracted with lesser individuals to provide a troop or section each. Skinner, from his H.Q. in Hansi, would provide the uniforms, saddlery and transport, the men bringing their own horses. At an appointed time the troops would report, join up with other troops and make up squadrons to form the regiment. They would drill and exercise until Skinner marched them to the army rendezvous; then, after manoeuvering under the eye of the General Staff, the army marched towards enemy territory and the battles that followed. At the end of the campaign the regiment returned to its district, where the men were disbanded and got on with their farm cropping. It was not until after the Mutiny (1857), when the Government of India decided to take over from the East India Company, that irregular corps became the regular units of the Indian Army.

When I first enrolled, the cavalry were still '*silladar*', that is to say, the regiments enrolled their own men, who brought along their own horses. They were provided with their uniforms and accoutrements, which were still at the choice of the C.O. - the individual soldier being cut a small amount each month from his pay until they were paid for. When he completed his service he received a refund. The system was abolished following the First World War when, with expansion, units were not able to come by the equipment that they required.

But in 1927, when Skinner's Horse moved station from Ferozepore to Loralai in Baluchistan, I, as Quarter-Master, had to arrange the provision of all our transport for the 1,000 mile trek, which took some twelve weeks. This transport included innumerable bullock carts for one stage of the journey, camels for another, possibly many riverboats, and back to bullock carts again: everything arranged with local contractors en route. Later on, we moved by rail, and had a regimental train to take the 600 men and horses and 800 or more followers - *syces*, barbers, farriers, armourers, etc. plus their wives and families. Indian officers were allowed to have their families with them; the men were not. By that time, in most stations, the men were housed in barracks, but in Jhelum the men shared one of a line of mud-built quarters and shared a *syce* (and the *syce's* wife)

Modern day application

Sir,

Your humble petitioner is poor man in agricultural behaviour and much depends on season for staff of life. Therefore, he throws himself upon his families bended knees and begs of mercifull consideration.

Your humble petitioner was too ill last rains and was taking vernacular medicine which made grand excavations in the coffers of your humble servant. That poor humble servant has large family of seven livers, two male and five female, last of whom is milking the parental mother, and another birth coming through grace of God to second wife of bosom. Therefore he prays that if there is a place ever so small in the back side of the honourable 64th Battery this humble slave be allowed to creep in, for which benevelence your humble servant will as in duty bound ever pray for your long life and prosperity.

Letter written by an ex-line *syce*
wishing to be re-engaged in the Battery.

(The work not of the syce, but of his village letter-writer, who probably charged him not less than four annas for this literary pearl.)

between them. The Indian Army then and thereafter was a model of organisation.

Colonel James Skinner was badly wounded in one encounter and lay on the ground as the tide of battle swept over him. That night he prayed that he might survive, and swore to God that if he did so he would build a Christian church, a mosque, and a Hindu temple. The romantic story has it that, at day-break, the daughter of the local village chief emerged with her woman to succour the fallen, she tended Skinner and nursed him back to health, following which he married her. In fact, Skinner with the rest of the wounded lay parched with thirst by day and frozen by night, and on the second morning they were tended by a low caste couple and finally brought in to the camp of the Rajput victor, who treated them kindly. Skinner rewarded the couple with 1,000 rupees. True to his vow, Skinner built the magnificent church in Old Delhi named St. James's after him, as well as a Hindu temple across the road and a Mohammedan mosque on his estate at Hansi, which had been given to him by a grateful government.

There was a famous character who was attached to the Indian State Forces. In the cold weather the Viceroy went on tour, and visited a number of Native States whose princes, to please the head of the government, provided wonderful tiger or small game shoots, such entertainment going a long way to acquiring a coveted decoration. One year, the tour included a very small state which housed no tiger, nor duck, nor sand grouse. All it had was a small lake in which resided an enormous *mahseer* fish. The fish was fed to bursting point at the hour when it was arranged for the Viceroy to fish for it. The catch was 100% certain. The Viceroy would be pleased to catch the record *mahseer*, and with luck the decoration would follow.

Unfortunately, no. One individual, unknown to the state officials, visited the lake a week before His Excellency, cast in his bait and after a monumental struggle landed the fish. No record *mahseer* for the Viceroy - in fact no *mahseer* at all and no decoration for the poor little Rajah.

* *

Times changed after the First World War. The officer establishment was reduced. There were five "axes" and, when anyone in the particular category under the axe stepped ever so slightly out of line, he found himself compulsorily retired. We all became good little boys and the swashbucklers of the old days were heroes of the past.

Not long after I arrived back from leave, there was trouble in the Doaba district of the Punjab, caused by a gang of recalcitrants, mostly ex-army Sikhs, who called themselves the Baba Akali. The movement was quasi-religious but was in fact revolutionary, and aimed at destroying law and order in that part of the countryside. Captained by an ex-*havildar* (infantry sergeant), Karam Singh by name, they murdered village headmen, plundered the villages and looted the money-lenders and bankers. They hid in the jungle and were highly mobile - appearing out of the blue to commit their crimes and then vanishing. Something had to be done. The police were unable to cope and the government ordered out two squadrons of both Skinner's and Hodson's Horse. The month was May and very hot indeed. We entrained the horses in a temperature of 110ö, eight horses to a wagon.

On arrival, we marched to our appointed location, the squadrons being some 15 miles apart. My seniors all being away on leave, I commanded 'C' Squadron. I picketed the squadron in a mango grove which provided dense shade, the men pitched their tents and I lived in a tiny rest house. Being out in the blue we were extremely short of stores; no butter, bread or green vegetables and no green fodder for the horses. On Day Three the Risaldar told me that the horses had started to eat the fallen mangoes. This I did not believe, but walking round 'stables' there was a plump, and down fell a mango. The nearest animal stretched out to the length of his heel rope, picked up the mango, masticated it with relish and spat out the stone. A mango fresh off the tree is a luscious fruit, very different from those bought in the shops or imported over here. At the start of the hot weather an Indian would sit down beside a heap of 100 or more mangoes and get through the lot, regarding this as a method of cleansing the stomach.

We marched the squadron round our area 'showing the flag', hoping to give confidence to the villagers, but how to capture the Baba Akalis? To start with, none of us knew what any of them looked like, but the police dug up a few informers who were reputed to recognise some of them by sight, and by promises of reward, information came in from time to time that the gang had been seen at, or were reputed to be going to visit, a certain village. We then went out after dark to surround the village before daybreak and, accompanied by the police, we made a drive though the village and had every male out of it, sat them down in a circle in an open space, and covered by rifles, the informers would search every face for the wanted men. I sometimes went up the tower of the mosque and watched the drive below; there was much squeaking and abuse of the beaters by the women and maybe a bit of "hanky-panky" as well to enliven the proceedings.

Having done the journey in the comparative cool of the night and sorted out the village, we started on the trek home by which time it was appallingly hot. Our camp was anything up to 25 miles away, and we took it very easily, walking the horses and stopping from time to time to water them and give them a feed which we carried in a feed bag attached to our saddles. I, on various occasions, drank my fill from a village well - a thing that one would never dream of doing normally for fear of enteric. Run down from lack of decent food, hot and exhausted, one was exactly in a state to pick up any germ going; luckily I contracted no illness.

It was all very romantic, on one's own and in command of a squadron. I could not, with only five years' service, have been happier. Every week, I or Basil Randall (later killed within yards of me on the polo ground in Lahore) visited each other and compared notes. Several times he arranged with a local 'big shot' to give us a 'blow out' - a tremendous supper of curry and *chupattis*, washed down with beer, and at the end of it, I and my escort mounted our horses and rode home belching loudly. We went straight across country under the starlit sky to be stopped by our camp sentries,

"Halt! Who goes there?"

"Friend."

"Advance friend and give the counter-sign."

Great fun and a fine meal under one's belt.

Neither we nor the other squadrons ever caught a Baba Akali, and nothing further was heard of the gang then. The temperature got progressively hotter before the approaching monsoon rains fell, and life got very boring. I longed for the cool of the hills and a spell of leave in which to enjoy it. One day the Commissioner of Jullundur arrived in my camp. A commissioner was a high up civil administrator, taking precedence over a major-general, and I was a junior captain. He asked me where I thought the gang had got to. The foothills of the Himalayas were only some forty miles to the north, and seeing my chance I replied that I thought it likely they had sought safety by making off into the mountains perhaps en route for central Asia. The big man considered.

"You may be right, my boy. Take some of your men and see if you can get any news of them."

The next day, leaving the Risaldar to hold the fort, I set out with a section and two pack animals. We crossed a mile-wide river bed, dry at that time of the year, and in two days were climbing into the hills. Though not yet high up it was marvellous to be out of the glare of the plains, the air getting fresher every mile. On day four, we came on a forest rest house, a cosy little thatched red-curtained bungalow, built out on a bluff with a splendid view back over the plains to the south. We decided to spend the night there. In the sitting-room was a pile of English weeklies. The first that I picked up was the Sunday Pictorial of 1901, with pictures of King Edward's coronation procession. The second issue of the same year was fronted by a photo:

"Lovely young girl charms all London by her dancing - Miss Phyllis Monckman, aged 17."

That was going back a bit, for Phyllis was still one of the big stars in musical comedy in 1923, along with Jack Buchanan, Heather Thatcher and Leslie Henson.

On again the next day, climbing all the way and meeting charming hill people who stared at the soldiers and the size of our horses. Then the tiny hill cattle standing barely 3ft high and as agile as cats - quite enchanting. That evening my section *daffadar* (sergeant) came to me and said:

"Sahib, the clouds are gathering. It must be the monsoon, and if the rains start we will never be able to get back across that river, which can rise 6 inches in an hour."

I realised he was right, and we had better head back. Sure enough the next day we had heavy showers, and on the following day it was raining torrents. I have known 8 inches of rain fall in three hours. We hurried. When we arrived at the river it was 300 yards of swiftly flowing water. No time to lose. One of the pack horses had my tin bath as a top load while the other had two goats that we had bought for rations. We took to the water, each horse helped by two kindly fisher folk. The water deepened to 2ft, 3ft. It was all the party could do to keep their feet. The goat pack-horse stumbled into a hole and fell, and was swept away with the wretched goats, bleeting piteously. God bless the *daffadar* - we would have been in a pretty pickle with a mile of water between us and the squadron. On our return, the mango grove was swamped out and the squadron had moved to higher and drier gound. A week later we were recalled to Ferozepore.

Come the cold weather we, as usual, started section training, followed by troop and then squadron and regimental training. These embraced both drill and field work. The cavalry drill area was a sea of dust, and when the regiment was drilling at the gallop, the dust was so thick that, literally, I could not see my horse's head or my hand in front of my face. Orders were given by bugle call and, mercifully, they were never misinterpreted; a squadron wheeling right when another wheeled left would have led to a monumental crash and pile-up. Men and horses came off parade white from head to foot, and the dust was sour and gritty in one's mouth. Apart from the dust, regimental drill parades were great fun; the blare of the bugles, the roar of 2,500 hoof beats and the jostle and scramble to keep one's position gave never a dull moment.

* *

The following spring there was trouble between two Native States, one very large, the other very small. The Nabob of the small one indulged in the hobby of abducting women and interning them in his harem. We were told how he sent photographers into his villages to photograph likely girls in the nude. This form of art was unheard of 50 years ago. His

Highness would thumb through the prints and his selections were removed from the bosom of their families for his personal use. If any of the family objected, they were clapped into prison, the cells of which consisted of what may be described as large graves. The covering gravestone had a hole in the top through which food for the internees was tipped. If the prisoner further voiced his objection, his gaolers were not above adding a scorpion to the day's ration. The Government of India often turned a blind eye, but there were limits.

The story goes that this enthusiastic old gentleman abducted a girl from his big neighbour's establishment by a ruse. He sent over a 'palace car' whose chauffeur was dressed in his neighbour's uniform. He had intrigued with one of the other inmates that the girl in question should opt for a drive, a quite normal procedure. They entered the car and drove off, but once clear of the palace grounds the driver put his foot down and raced for the State border. The Maharaja who owned the girl was furious at his loss, and threatened that if she was not returned forthwith he would march in his State army and recapture her. The Government of India could not countenance a private war. The outcome was that the abducting Rajah was deposed, and Skinner's Horse marched in to preserve order. We arrived to find that we shared a mess with an infantry battalion. The first evening, one of their seniors, having collected a gin and bitter, turned to the assembled company and proposed

"Well, tight ... (followed by a rude word)"

We were not amused. After all the officers' mess was the officers' mess, where, incidentally, it was a rigid convention that the name of a woman was never mentioned. We were not prudes; it was just a code of behaviour and the fellow was, we thought, showing off in front of his obvious betters!

A civil commissioner was appointed to settle the affairs of the little State. One of his headaches was how to de-mob the 120 or so girls, who, ravished by the Nabob, were not all that acceptable back in the family circle. How the poor fellow went about it, and whatever the outcome, was no affair of ours, and in due course we returned to our lines in Ferozepore.

From there I went on my first long leave, after six years' service.

The following year (1925), I was posted to the Adjutantcy of the Viceroy's Bodyguard, while the incumbent was on long leave (eight months). I then had seven years' service, and the early attraction of routine life in the cavalry had palled somewhat. So it was thrilling to join the crack unit of the Indian Army, even if in a temporary capacity; added to that the Commandant was Joey Atkinson, the captain of the last polo team to play the Americans, a hero if ever there was one.

The Bodyguard were in the summer station of Dehra Dun, having moved up there in April from Delhi. Dehra Dun lies at the foot of the Mussoorie hills and is some 3,000ft so it is fairly cool. Every trooper stood over 6ft, each with a magnificent beard. Their Indian officers displayed a tremendous presence and held their own in any company. The horses were selected for their size and good looks. A grandson of James Skinner lived in Mussoorie and Joey, who was a very keen shot, told me to visit him and see if he could lend us his elephant on which we could shoot the Viceroy's jungles, which were close to Dehra. I duly called on the old man. He was a nice old boy, full of his own importance and his value to the Empire, and wrote regularly to the King.

He explained that the elephant had died, but showed me a fine armoury of guns and rifles, the gem of which was a beautifully chased .303 double-barrelled rifle, which of course fired army ammunition. He had married, secondly, a Scots girl by whom he had a son. My visit was not entirely fruitless as he had a niece known as 'The Cobra', a very sophisticated young lady, educated in Paris, and with whom I went to several dance parties.

* *

The following year I went as A.D.C. to the Viceroy. What a change were my sumptuous quarters in Viceregal Lodge, Delhi, from the tumbledown mud bungalows in Ferozepore! How dashing the A.D.C.s and how they were courted by the hostesses of the capital. The Viceroy of the day was Rufus Isaacs, Lord Reading, who first landed in India as a cabin boy on a freighter and, on his next visit, to the blare of bands and guards of honour as Viceroy designate of India. He was a man of extraordinary capability. Sitting at his dinner table, I gazed enthralled at a face which depicted his masterful personality and peerless intelligence. When it was my turn to be A.D.C. on duty, my first act was to accompany him on his early morning ride. I rode respectfully, half a horse's length behind him. He seldom spoke, engrossed no doubt with the many problems that beset his position. It was a time when Indian politicians aspired to self-government. By custom they were labelled 'agitators' by the British and 'patriots' by the Indians, and great men some of them were - Ghandi, Nehru and, later, Jinnah. They spent considerable periods of time in gaol for rabble-rousing.

At that time the Viceroys lived in Old Delhi. New Delhi, planned by the famous architect Lutyens, was in the course of construction. I was on the staff during Lord Reading's last week of office, and on a brilliant moon-lit night we accompanied him on a tour of the half-completed new Viceroy's house, a palace of red sandstone. To the south the gardens were taking shape, while to the north stretched the two mile approach, King's Way, tree-lined and bordered by grass lawns which were bordered again by water-ways, and beyond them another avenue of trees. We moved on to the fort built by the Moghuls, three miles away. The scene could not have been more romantic, as in the bright moonlight we strolled through the marble interior and looked out over the vast *maidan* (open space) towards the 'Old Fort' and the Jamma Masjid, the largest place of worship of the Muslims in all India. There, every Friday, the day of prayer, tens of thousands gathered in the courtyard, according to custom.

Much to my disappointment my C.O. requested my return to act as his Quarter-master; I think he considered it was not good for a young officer to bask among the fleshpots for too long. Back in the regiment again we entered for the Lahore
one more page !!!! Christmas Polo Tournament and won it. I was becoming a proficient player, and many were the congratulations after the final. I was a very proud young man. We had played Probyn's Horse in the final, and in the last of the six chukkers, an opponent swung his stick to hit the ball to the left: the stick whipped round his pony's neck and struck me, riding alongside him, full across the face. The head of a polo stick of 52 inches of whippy cane, which can drive a polo ball

100 yards, strikes a terrible blow. This stroke broke my nose and knocked me out and, having fallen off my pony, I found myself on my knees streaming blood on the turf, and my pony, a light grey, looked as though he had been hit by a charge of grape shot. I had a black eye for a week, but my handicap that year was raised to 6.

Shortly after this I was offered the Adjutantcy of the Governor of Bombay's Bodyguard - another crack unit. The regiment was off to Baluchistan with no polo in view and my C.O., who was relinquishing command, allowed me to take the job. The Adjutantcy was a three-year appointment and life was really looking up.

* * * * *

D.H. when Adjutant of the Governor's Bodyguard, Bombay.

CHAPTER VII

BOMBAY

I travelled down to Bombay on the Frontier Mail arriving at 7 am, and was met by a Government House car, the driver dressed in white uniform with a scarlet chest piece - very grand. It was mid-February and the air was delightfully warm and moist after the raw dust of the Punjab. Government House is situated on a point running out into the vast expanse of Bombay harbour and there is usually a light breeze from one direction or another. The grounds with trees and flowers were beautifully kept and the lawns and paths watered early each morning. They formed an ideal setting for the white-painted buildings which housed H.E.'s and the staff quarters, the offices and the main entertaining block. The quarters were sited just above the sea shore, and from their verandahs one looked down at the rippling water 20 feet below. I was given rooms which might have been planned for a film star - a large bedroom with two french windows leading on to a long verandah, and a luxurious bathroom with a marble bath. When I returned to change in the evenings, there would be waiting a dry martini. The establishment stood us food and drink, and we could buy a bottle of first class champagne (out of bond to G.H.) for Rs.10 (13 shillings).

His Excellency the Governor at that time was Sir Leslie Wilson, a one time Royal Marine, and his staff consisted of a Private Secretary (civilian), his doctor, a military secretary and four or five A.D.C.s, all serving officers; his Bodyguard Commandant and its Adjutant. The A.D.C.s in rotation did a day's duty with His Excellency, Her Excellency (The Governor's wife), house guests, and 'in waiting', ie. on call for extra duty.

The Governor had to do a considerable amount of entertaining among the Civil, military and business communities, and had a constant flow of guests passing through Bombay, those arriving by ship (there was of course no air travel in

The Bombay Bodyguard, 1927.

L to R: Senior Risaldar Nathud Singh
Major Hugh Lucas - Cammandant
Captain Denzil Holder - Adjutant
Jamadar Ahmed Khan

those days) en route to the capital Delhi, or to Calcutta. These were met by Government House white-uniformed '*Putti Wallas*' (house servants) outside their cabins, who took charge of the luggage and escorted them to waiting G.H. cars.

Dinner parties were for fifty-two - the number that the table sat - and the A.D.C.s in waiting had the job of introducing each guest, when His Excellency and his consort arrived. The invitation office had produced a list of the guests, each in his order of precedence. The A.D.C. had to memorise the lot, recognise each of them on arrival, and range them round the room in correct order. The arrivals included British, Indians and Parsees - the last named having completely tongue-twisted names such as Danjiboy, Degeboy and worse, and if the A.D.C. was new or did not know them he had little time to fit faces to names before H.E. entered. He could never be certain in the babel of conversation and gossip that some of them would not change places. Although I helped out as an extra A.D.C. I was never involved in the introduction.

While life was pretty busy, there was any amount of recreation. Several of the staff played our three days a week polo; His Excellency had two tennis courts going most days and guests in to play. The staff shared a very fast yacht moored at the superbly appointed Yacht Club, who promoted races every Saturday. There was horse racing at the magnificent Bombay Race Club course at Mahalaxmi. The Jackal Club hunted every Sunday and the Gymkhana Club provided every known ball game - cricket, rugger, hockey, tennis and squash. I have never met a place where so many different sports could be indulged in.

At the approach of the hot weather all the Seats of Government left the plains for the cool of the hills; the Viceroy to Simla, Calcutta to Darjeeling, Madras to Ooty. Bombay did three moves - to Bombay from November to February, then to Mahbleshwar until the rains broke when we moved down to Poona until the following November. The Bodyguard did Bombay and up to Poona.

My Commandant, Major Hugh Lucas, was a brilliant horseman and polo player and, in the past, had been a top class steeplechase jockey. On the polo field he played No.3 to my 2 and with two indifferent A.D.C.s, we lifted all the local cups in

The Bombay Bodyguard Polo Team

L to R: Hugh Lucas Denzil Holder Indian A.D.C. Jackie Cryer

Bombay and Poona. Hugh was also an exceptional horse-master and trainer of raw polo ponies, and during the three years we were together, he passed on much of his skills to me.

In 1928 we planned to join up with Joey Atkinson and Claude Pert (both internationals) and enter for the Indian Polo Association championship, to be played at Christmas in Calcutta. At the last moment Hugh had to pull out but, with great generosity and trust, lent me his two best polo ponies. David Davison filled in for Hugh and we won the championship - one of the few occasions when the trophy was not won by one or other of the top Indian State teams: Jodhpur, Jaipur, Bhopal or Kashmir.

We took the enormous championship cup to Firpo's - Calcutta's top restaurant - that night, where we were greeted by a roll from the dance band drums. There entered a procession led by two waiters, then Firpo himself preceding four more waiters carrying a jeroboam of champagne in a vast cooler. I cannot remember how many pints go to a jeroboam but more than enough to give us and our friends a hilarious evening.

The Bodyguard was composed of two troops - one Mohammedan and the other Sikh. They were a fine looking body of men, all bearded and standing over six feet. Their duties consisted of doing dismounted sentry duty at G.H. at both entrances and on the main buildings, and forming a mounted escort when H.E. performed some special function in the town, or when he drove in state up the Race Course at Bombay and at Poona. Our mounts, some seventy in number, were largely thoroughbreds off the race course - given to us by their owners when they had got to the top of the handicap. The Bodyguard lines were only a step from the race course, and had a splendid pillared entrance, barracks for the men, a stable block for the horses and a fine riding school in the centre. There were may trees and flowerbeds.

The Bodyguard paraded for an hour daily under the Indian officers, trained a few of the last joined remounts, and Hugh's and my orderlies schooled our polo ponies. We also ran a riding school for those wanting to learn to ride or requiring gentle exercise in safe surroundings, for which a charge was made, which went towards augmenting Bodyguard funds. When on duty the men wore a ten yard long gold fronted red turban, scarlet *Kurtha* (long tunic) with shoulder chains, white breeches, black top boots and white gauntlets. On a racecourse drive, mounted on our splendid animals, they presented a magnificent spectacle with their lance pennants fluttering in the breeze, outriders in front, a troop before and behind H.E.'s carriage, and the Commandant and Adjutant at each side of the carriage. Our turnout was as good or better than that of the British Household Cavalry; we even varnished our horses' hooves. On these occasions H.E. wore grey morning dress and the accompanying A.D.C.s donned white drill tunics and overalls, a spiked helmet and swords slung from a gold belt.

We had one very showy horse, Briksworth, an English thoroughbred presented by Sir Victor Sassoon. Briksworth was one of the pair of 'points' that headed the procession on these drives and was very much admired.

Sir Leslie Wilson was no horseman but a very handsome, proud individual who enjoyed his status, his surroundings, and his staff, and he much admired Briksworth, the only animal whose name he knew. One year, while we were in Poona, Briksworth lost condition owing probably to the fact that it was very difficult to get green fodder for the horses during the hot weather. Hugh was a great believer in giving such a case a saline stomach wash. McElligot, the vet, was summoned and he did the necessary with a stirrup pump that put the saline solution into the animal's stomach direct, through a rubber tube. He instructed our "veterinary assistant" as how to repeat the operation. Care had to be taken to ensure that the tube, passing through the horse's mouth, went into the right passage. The following day Bishan Singh, our own man, went through the motions but allowed the tube to pass into Briksworth's windpipe and thereby into his lungs. He collapsed - drowning. McElligot was phoned and arrived hot foot, applied mustard plasters, but Briksworth was very shortly dead. This was a great loss in itself but what appalled us was that in two days' time His Excellency was due to perform his annual inspection of the B.G.

What to do? What indeed!

While we were pondering this problem Risaldar Natha Singh whispered to Hugh,

"Sahib, Battleaxe is very like Briksworth!"

Battleaxe was put into Briksworth's stall, under his name plate.

The daimler arrived, Hugh and I, in our best white uniforms saluted, and the Royal Salute was blown by the trumpeter.

"Good morning Hugh, good morning Denzil - lovely day. How's Briksworth?"

"I think you will find all is well, Sir," said Hugh, walking up to No.1 stall.

"By Jove he is looking well."

Hugh and I looked at each other and breathed sighs of relief.

His Excellency was later in serious trouble with Mahatma Gandhi's Congress Party's "civil disobedience" campaign which, blown up by inflammatory speeches of trained agitators, could explode at any moment into local, if not all-India, revolution. The wealth of Bombay lay in its cotton mills, which employed tens of thousands of mill workers. They were miserable little specimens compared to our northerners but, when set alight, they could be as cruel, vicious and dangerous as any lot anywhere. During my time there was serious rioting. I cannot remember its cause - if there was one - but I can tell you that a rioter could be bought for threepence a day. These were anti-Mohammedan and the mob set about the comparatively few Pathans employed as night watchmen. They were big, powerful men; but what chance had a Goliath when surrounded and attacked by a mob of mill hands. Scores of them were cut down and battered to death, often hacked to pieces and shoved down man-holes.

When Edward, Prince of Wales visited India in 1921 he was met on the quay in Bombay by anti-British (3d. a day) pickets with banners telling him to "go home". The police and troops, brought in for the occasion, had all they could do to bring him safely to Government House. There was a running battle in the streets - all four miles of them - and at the end of the day it was said of one Gurkha Battalion that no man came back to camp with a clean bayonet. H.R.H., with his accustomed light touch, cabled his father, King George V,

"Tremendous reception stop. 500 killed stop. Edward."

For the British Raj, which had held sway for 150 years, the writing was on the wall - although it took nearly thirty years to come about.

It was popular among the Labour Party's left, and also among Americans, to decry the position of the British in India, backing the screams of India's Congress Party, "Imperialist exploitation - grinding the faces of the poor into the dust". In fact the British did a wonderful job in India. Some 2,000 or so British Civil Servants, Political Officers in native states, judges, officers of the canal, forestry and medical services held the continent together in peace and security, with justice and impartiality of race, religion and wealth. You must remember that India, in those days, included both today's Hindu India and Mohammedan Pakistan, and its 400 million inhabitants spoke some thirty different languages. The peoples of the Punjab in the north were as different from those of Madras in the south as those of the U.K. and Turkey. Furthermore, many very large and quite tiny native states occupied a third of India's land space.

Perhaps the greatest benefit conferred on the peoples of India was that of security, enabling them to go about their daily business with peace of mind. A further benefit was our irrigation works that brought vast tracts of desert into cultivation: famines were practically a disaster of the past. Medical services and hospitals did much to alleviate distress and curb diseases - cholera, plague and the like. Hard-working District Officers toured the country-side in tented camps and settled grievances and local disputes and linked the ordinary man with the local and central government. The outcome of their efforts was that the peasants, who formed 90% of the population, lived contented lives and had tremendous trust and respect for the Sahibs. They approached us as '*Hazoor*' - 'Your Honour', and 'Protector of the Poor'. The only dissenting voice came from the politicians and lawyers, some of whom were idealists but mostly, I think, those who smelt well paid jobs then held by the British.

In eastern countries graft is endemic, but the British had no part in this. It was, I was told, commonplace in the compounds of the Law Courts for auctions to be held between counsels for the services of a witness. The Indians loved litigation and would ruin themselves to win a suit, usually borrowing the money to do so. Usury, forbidden to Mohammedans, was a curse in India. Money-lenders would offer credit but at an extortionate rate of interest, and not only to the Indians. In the old days it was commonplace for young officers to go to the *Bania* for ready cash, and there were numerous cases of quite senior officers being smuggled out of their station and out of the country to avoid their inability to settle their debts. Every regiment had its money-lenders and when the Central India Horse were in Jhelum I talked to their *Bania* - a very nice old man who told me in 1920:

"The Sahibs to-day are a poor lot and only come to me for a few hundred rupees or so, whereas in the old days there were real gentlemen who owed me 30,000 rupees and - look you - he had twenty polo ponies and each pony a gold martingale. Those were the days!"

I asked him - did he get paid?

"Good heavens no. The Sahib was killed pig sticking. A great Sahib that - a real Central India Horseman."

The C.I.H., who in their maroon jerseys won the India Cavalry and inter-regimental polo tournaments on many occasions, were the amalgamated 38th and 39th regiments of the Central India Horse, which were both stationed permanently in Central India at the two stations of Auga and Goona and, every so often, swapped stations. Both lay in excellent tiger country and tiger-shooting was one of their main preoccupations. They enlisted expert *shikaris* who, in the season, spent much of their time scouring the nearby jungles to get news of a tiger kill. Should one of them come back with the news of a kill, even during a regimental parade, soldiering was abandoned then and there, and a quick change was made into shooting kit and away to a tiger hunt.

The tiger, having killed, eats a portion of the corpse - probably a deer or a villager's cow - and lies up nearby for a snooze before returning for the rest of his meal. A beat is then arranged around the area of the kill and *machans* (platforms in trees) constructed for the guns. The guns in place, 100 or so villagers beating tin cans would advance towards the line of *machans*. The top *shikari* - one of their Indian officers - would sense, with unerring skill, the route that the tiger, angrily disturbed from his sleep, would take, and he would place his Colonel Sahib Bahadur in the *machan* overlooking its path. This

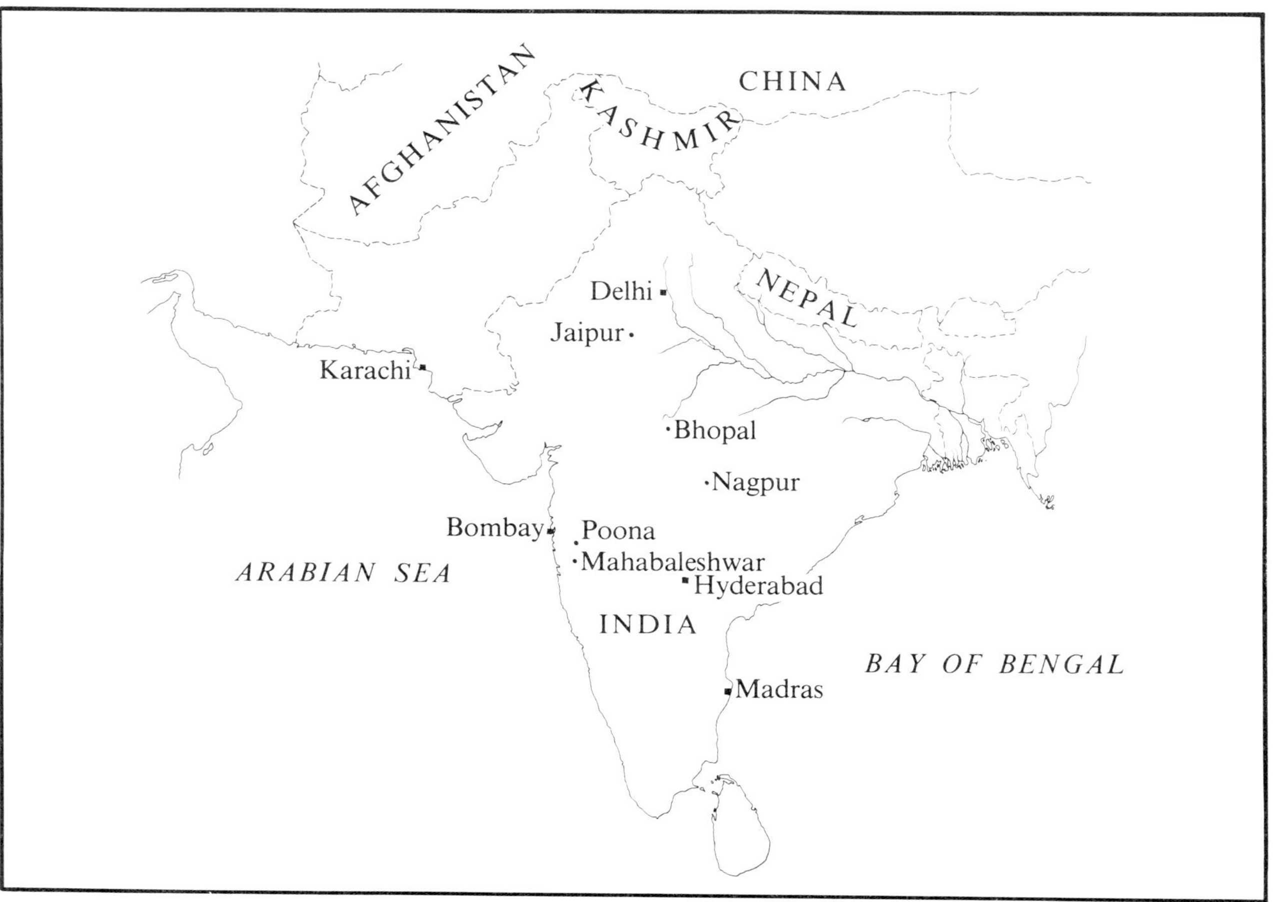
AFGHANISTAN
KASHMIR
CHINA
NEPAL
Delhi
Jaipur
Karachi
Bhopal
Nagpur
Bombay
Poona
Mahabaleshwar
Hyderabad
ARABIAN SEA
INDIA
BAY OF BENGAL
Madras

did not always work out but most often it did. Colonel Capper, who commanded the C.I.H. when they came up to Jhelum, had bagged 28 tigers - many of these during his term of command.

Indians were compulsive gamblers, and the Saturday races provided them with a splendid opportunity to have a flutter. The top race courses were situated in Calcutta, Bombay and, to a lesser degree, Madras, while there were a number of tracks in large military stations throughout the country. Each of the top courses, being some 1,000 miles apart, maintained its own training establishments, and the trainers in the main ran their horses on their local tracks. Stabled in Bombay were some 800 English and Australian horses and 1,000 Arabs. Several agencies produced a weekly publication detailing previous races in which the entrants had run, along with dates, distances, weights and placings etc. from the study of which the student of form could make a fair estimate of his particular selection's chances.

* *

Bombay, like all eastern ports, was hot and muggy, and one took one's exercise in the cool of the morning. My day started when I was woken at 5.15 am - into uniform and into my car. The way led over Malabar Hill, where the millionaires had their palaces. I aimed to pass the top a minute or two each side of 6 am when down below one looked on the curving boulevard of Back Bay, still lit up by a string of electric lights, the sea a sheet of silver. On the far side of the bay and behind a line of black hills, the dawn was breaking in marvellous hues of scarlet and gold. Often the moon and a few of the brighter stars still shone. It was a wonderful sight and I marvelled at it every time I passed.

During the monsoon, June and July, the stables moved up from the steamy heat of Bombay to Poona, some 40 miles distant on a plateau, 2,000 feet high, where racing continued. One race day an extraordinary thing happened. A completely unknown Arab won his race. The immense electric tote board showed the number of tickets taken on each runner. When this entry won all eyes turned to the board and there, to everyone's astonishment, only one ticket was registered - the odds 14,000 to one. Quite a crowd hurried to the pay-out windows to see

The game of 'Sahibs & Rajahs'

who had been the successful punter. It turned out to be a *bhisti* - a menial water carrier - the fellow who produced one's bath water. What had happened was that this *bhisti* had dreamed that this number would win. He could not afford Rs.10 - nearly his month's wages - so he went round the compound servants to raise the price of the ticket.

As the *bhisti* approached the pay out window a cheer went up. The window clerk told him that the tote could not pay out the sum of the winnings right away but "Here was 4,000 rupees and come back after the last race", when they would give him a cheque for 10,000. Well, here was 4,000 rupees - riches beyond belief. He held his cotton skirt beneath the window and the clerk shovelled the paper notes into it. The *bhisti* folded the ends of his skirt about the notes, turned round and collapsed - dead. The shock had been too much for him. Onlookers pressed forward to help the poor fellow to his feet and in the scrimmage which ensued more than half the cash found its way into the pockets of the helpers.

An Indian cavalry regiment keen on polo could not afford to let its officers keep race horses and indulge in racing. It wanted all their efforts and cash invested in polo ponies for the regimental team. If a fellow wanted to race he was requested to remove his enthusiasm elsewhere. We needed every one of our officers to compete with the British Cavalry.

In the autumn of 1928 the Maharajah Hamidulla of Bhopal, a 9 handicap player, asked Hugh and I to spend ten days in his State and play polo. Hugh could not get away but kindly sent me off. Bhopal had also got hold of Dalrymple Hay of the C.I.H. (8 h'cap) and the Jodhpur cracks, Hanut Singh and Prithi Singh (both 9 h'cap). We four were to oppose the Bhopal team to tune them up before the coming championships. We had a wonderful time there and of course first class polo. The polo ground at Bhopal was on black cotton soil which granulated into small pea sized lumps and formed an extraordinarily smooth surface which remained so for about six chukkers (each 7½ minutes). After that we had a break, while an elephant drew a brush harrow over the ground (300 x 150 yards) and smoothed it out for further play.

I was put to play No.1 for our team and, during our matches there, hardly missed a shot at goal. The rules of polo state "The side wins that shoots the most goals" and hitting goals at polo, rather like sinking putts at golf, wins a lot of matches. Hamidulla was no obese, pleasure loving potentate but, small in stature and light in weight, was solid whipcord and took endless trouble to keep himself in peak condition. To this end, in one of the palace rooms, he had a ton or more of sand placed and, clothed in a singlet and grasping a spade, he shifted the sand from one side of the chamber to the other. This was followed by a steam bath and a rub down. He was gone over by his doctor daily and before polo always took a hot bath to relax his considerable muscles. His fellow Princes dubbed him 'The Coolie' - which passed over his head, the proof of the pudding coming when they met on the polo field.

Bhopal being a Mohammedan State was 'dry' and, while we drank very little, we did feel the need for a little something at the end of a day's hard exercise. We conspired with one of the Nabob's A.D.C.s and enquired if we might be allowed some beer. This was smuggled into our guest house, and we played all the better for it. We were shown the Nabob's tiger-shooting 'pit'. This was a small *nullah* not far from the palace. The sides were vertical, some 30 feet in height, and built in one side was a barred cage let into the rock. Prior to the arrival of a V.I.P. to whom a tiger was to be offered, the *nullah* would be baited with a goat or worn-out cow. The guest would 'sit up' over the bait inside the cage - where he was perfectly safe - and take the shot if the tiger appeared.

I am very grateful to Hamidulla for the many kindnesses that he showed me. He was not all sport; for years he was President of the Chamber of Princes that represented the Indian States' interests in the Government of India in Delhi, in which the Princes had a considerable say.

* *

During service in the east the most important factor to well-being was one's 'bearer', who was the personal servant, valet and butler. It was he who did the rooms, had ready the clothes to be worn, prepared the bath and waited on one in mess. Up country our servants were usually good chaps, especially in Indian regiments since we spoke their language and knew how to treat them - which was not always the case in British regiments. Government House did not fancy outside servants and kept a pool of bearers in which they had complete confidence. On arrival, I was told to return my Punjabi bearer and was allotted one by the name of Ganoo. He was tiny - 5 feet and about 50 years old, weighed about 7 stone and wore gold spectacles. I called him 'The Professor'.

He and the other G.H. staff were always pictures of neatness in their white drill suits, which were pressed daily. In India one never wore a garment that had not been newly pressed. This was accomplished by liaison between one's bearer and the *dhobi* (washer-man) who collected the worn garments - uniform, polo kit, underwear, socks - etc. and, if necessary, had them back the next morning.

Ganoo, like his kind, was super efficient. He spoke excellent English and had 'bearered' scores of the English nobility and V.I.P.s who visited India in the cold weather for sport or business of state. Before the advent of air travel they all landed in Bombay - the "Gateway of India" - from off the P & O vessels. They were met off the ship at the docks and during their stay were attended by the 'A.D.C.-guests'. Usually G.H. bearers relinquished their duty to their Sahib when he finished his tour of duty, but Ganoo and I were very attached to each other and, at the end of my three years, he came along with me to Lucknow. Shortly after my arrival there I acquired a canary, which Ganoo doted on. The bird was known as 'Canary Sahib' and when we motored to polo tournaments Ganoo treasured the cage on his knee. On one occasion, going to play polo in the championships in Calcutta, I was to stay in the home of a wealthy '*box walla*' (business man). I could not very well take 'Canary Sahib' along there and left him in charge of a friend. On my return I learnt that the poor little bird had been attacked in his cage - hung in a tree outside the bungalow - by a crow, and killed. Ganoo was heartbroken.

Servants on the whole were pretty honest, but during one's service there is no doubt one lost a lot of clothing and gear. Each year in Calcutta I bought a dozen thick, silk handkerchiefs - price one rupee. By the end of the year they had all gone. I do not think the bearer was the culprit, it was the *dhobi* and one was at fault to have blamed the bearer. A top class bearer was paid Rs.40 (£3.00) a month in those days. Could it be expected that the poor fellow would not purloin some small articles occasionally from the wealthy Sahib to help feed a family of maybe five or more children? The syces (grooms) got 13 rupees a month. Our troopers - fed and housed - got 25. Ranting, one day, about the idiocy of some soldiers, one of my seniors said:

"Denzil, he is only a Rs.25 man. Do not expect too much of him".

Looking back, I wish I had given my staff just that extra rupee or so which would have made such a difference to them and so little to me. Do not we all have regrets in our lives? I certainly have and am humbled by them.

* *

After the Bombay season ended in March, Government House moved up to Mahabaleshwar (5,000ft). There was practically no entertaining, His Excellency might have a few friends for a week-end, but that was all. We spent our time playing tennis spent our time playing tennis and hacking about the many paths among the rocky hills and enjoying the comparative cool. It was a great place for beautiful tree orchids which grew rather like mistletoe on the lichen-covered trees and hung down in a spray above the hill paths. The soil there was a deep brick colour - colourful in itself but not very attractive when there was little contrasting colour. When the monsoon broke with a dramatic drop in temperature we moved down to Poona. We lived at Ganeshkind, in a large park some four miles out of the town. The house was smaller than that in Bombay and built in a very formal style of stone. The B.G. lines were a mile away on the far side of the Park. The polo ground was in Poon itself. Polo was much better there than in Bombay, where we were hard put to get eight players at times, as there was a Cavalry regiment and a large garrison. There was a very fine race course and the Turf Club alongside it. The club subscription was pretty stiff and the members were mostly Bombay business men up for the week-end. The soldiers belonged to the Gymkhana Club - where they got all their games including polo. If I remember correctly the G.H. staff were made honorary members of both. We had a pretty good team one year as Errol Prior-Palmer (9th Lancers) joined the staff and, in a tremendous final in the big tournament, we beat Bhopal.

Poona sported one of the few hunts in India. We hunted every Sunday morning - meeting at 6 a.m. and, on many occasions, I dragged myself awake after only a few hours' sleep following a dance the night before and motored to the meet, where our B.G. horses would be waiting. We drew patches of sugar cane which usually provided a jackal or one of the small grey foxes that abounded. The latter usually ran in a circle but the jackals would head for a point many miles away and gave us a splendid hunt. On one occasion we started with a field of 94 and finished with only six. We covered 24 miles off the map and probably many more on the ground. I think we changed jacks twice but finally one made for a rocky hillock with the Master shouting to the survivors to head him off as hounds were on their last legs. The survivors were Hugh and I, both on English thoroughbreds, the Master and his whip, who had remounted, and two girls on two Arabs. They had been left miles in the rear half-way but their plucky little stayers were there all right at the finish. In the end the jack beat us to the hill - and we turned for home. We had covered some very rocky ground and I think we had only twelve shoes left between us. My horse Fujiama was out of it for a month.

I had a very lucky escape from losing an eye out hunting. An animal in front threw up a sharp grit which hit my left eye. I rubbed it and thought no more about it. Two or three days later Hugh asked me why I was rubbing my eye. I did not realise that I was doing so but, shortly after, the eye became very inflamed and painful. There was a tournament due in ten days time, and Hugh advised me to see H.E.'s surgeon. He gave me some drops - which stung like hell and were apparently the worst possible treatment, so Hugh phoned the military hospital and very luckily they had an eye surgeon who had just done a two year opthalmic course in Germany. I went down to see him. He put me in a black cloth cubicle and turned a miniature electric light on the eye. I saw the surgeon purse his lips and he told me that the face of the eye had been cut and was sloughing away to the rim. It wanted immediate attention. He told me I could see a world famous specialist in Bombay or he would have a go. He gave me such confidence that I told him to go ahead - whereupon he cocained the eye and, with a tiny instrument, cut the damaged face of the eye away until he got to clean skin. A dressing, and both eyes were bandaged up. A G.H. car fetched me back to G.H., I being led by the hand. The next day I went down again, into the cubicle and the surgeon took a long look. He asked me how I had slept and I told him not very well.

"Nor did I", he replied, "I thought that you were going to lose that eye" -

but the clean skin had spread a thin film of new skin which had covered the part which he had removed and in a week it was all right and, for thirteen years afterwards, when I lost it during the 1939 war in Eritrea - pierced by a mortar splinter.

At the end of the season came the hunt Point-to-Points and it had long been a matter of principle for the B.G. to win the Open Race. Hugh had a wonderful brown mare Dorothy - who had won the race twice before - and I a young Australian, Donald, that I had bought for the B.G. in Calcutta the year before. We were always rather frightened that a little vet from Bombay, Gerald McElligot, might have something up his sleeve to beat us. McElligot was a wonderful judge of a horse and he later became head of the British Bloodstock Agency in London had purchased for their clients animals that won several of the classics both here and abroad. I took Donald round the course the previous week and studied carefully a sharp descent into the last jump. The usual route down was very stony and steep and one had to take a pull approaching it but I reckoned that, by going further out, the incline was more gradual and better going and could be taken much faster. I decided to take it. On the day, we started a field of nine. I kept Donald about fifth with Hugh and McElligot well up in front. Three jumps out Hugh and I went into the lead and, going flat out, we came to the last decline. I swung out to the right and Hugh with me, then he called

"Denzil, we are too far out"

and turned back to the left. I galloped on without checking, and gained four or five lengths. Thinking I was safe I eased up at the last jump and paid for my discretion - Hugh came up with a rush, passed me at the jump and went on to win. I could not get mine going again. I was a mug. Dorothy was a wonderful mare but was getting on in years and I am sure that Donald was the better of the two on that day. It was I who lost him the race.

* * * * *

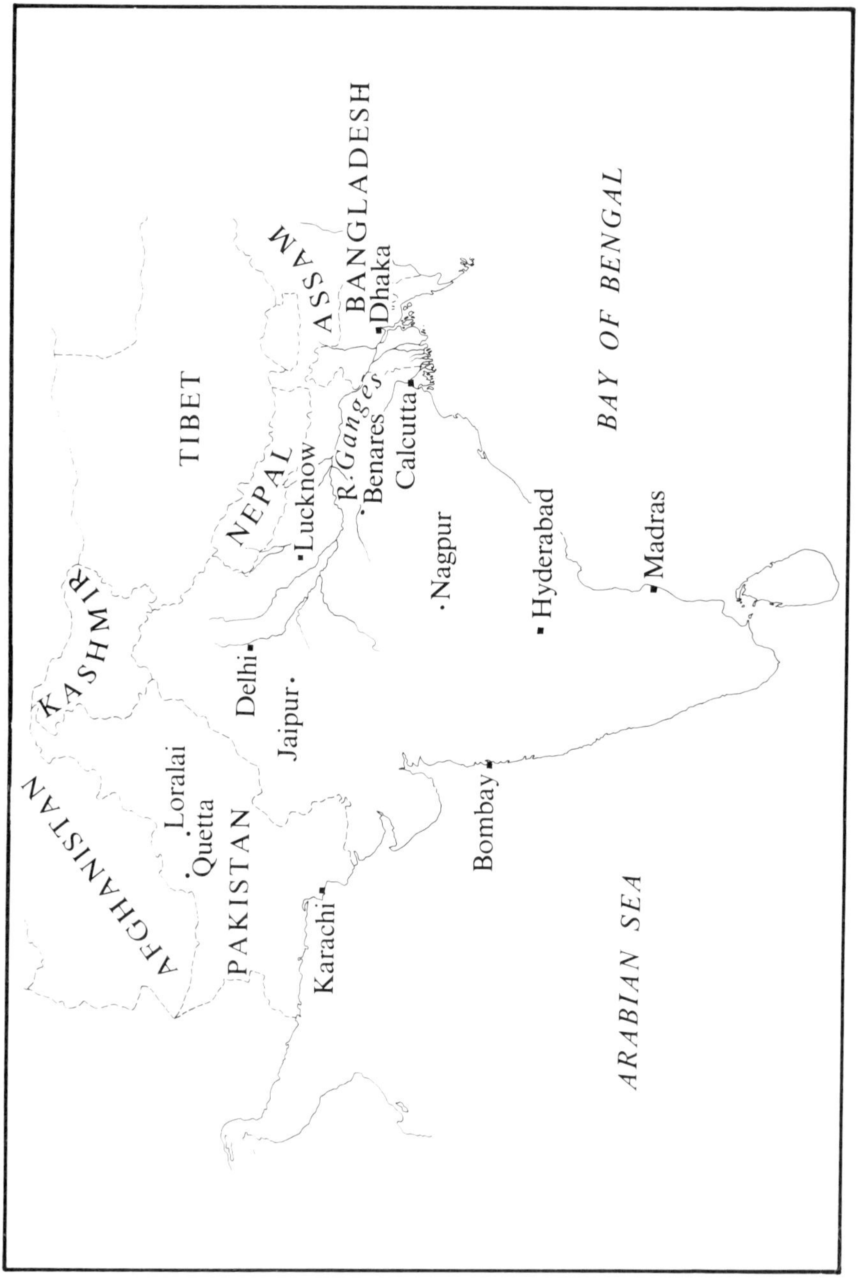

TIBET
NEPAL
ASSAM
BANGLADESH
KASHMIR
AFGHANISTAN
PAKISTAN
BAY OF BENGAL
ARABIAN SEA
R. Ganges
Dhaka
Calcutta
Benares
Lucknow
Delhi
Jaipur
Nagpur
Hyderabad
Madras
Bombay
Karachi
Quetta
Loralai

Lucknow: Northern India

CHAPTER VIII

L U C K N O W

The regiment had moved from Loralai, (only a two year station), to Lucknow, and my C.O. demanded my return to stiffen up the polo team. He told me to bring back a charger. In one of the big training stables was a celebrated and beautiful Indian bred grey named Steel Blue - a wonder horse whose performance had worked him up from Division 4 to Division 1, and in which he had won many good races, which at that time was unheard of for an Indian bred horse. He was then six years old and finished with racing.

Speaking to Natha Singh, the Bodyguard Risaldar (Senior Indian Officer) he told me that there might be a chance of my acquiring Steel Blue and he would make enquiries. Steel Blue - I could not believe it! Sure enough he arranged that the animal would be sent round to the Bodyguard lines one evening for me to try. He rode like a dream with a mouth like silk and a lovely loping thoroughbred action. I have never before or since experienced such poetry of motion. After expressing my pleasure to the Risaldar he said:

"Sahib, put him in your stable and he is yours."

Millionaire Victor Sassoon, who owned one of the biggest stables in Bombay, seventy or more animals, had offered me a magnificent bright bay horse which would have won the charger class in any horse show and in any company. While I dallied, waiting for a ride on him, Steel Blue's connections, who had had a poor run, went to a soothsayer who told them:

"You are about to part with a valued possession. Cancel this and your luck will return."

Valued possession? What could this be but Steel Blue? Had I kept the horse three days before I would have had the most perfect animal that could fall to one's lot to possess. I made up my mind never to hedge or dither again. The Almighty, a good friend to me all my life (although I did not always appreciate it at the time), had given me my chance and I had thrown it away. To the real cavalier, horse flesh was the most important thing in his life even (not always) transcending the love of women. The desert Arabs have a saying "Man can only be truly happy with his favourite mare between the knees - or between the knees of his favourite woman'. The majority of my best ponies were mares. They gave one something, some response that a gelding didn't. A rapport between the sexes? The Arabs never sold their mares, which were their pride and also their breeding stock.

* *

Lucknow was one of the largest stations in India, the garrison consisting of a British and an Indian cavalry regiment, two British and two Indian Infantry battalions, and a regiment of Artillery. It was the capital of the United Provinces and housed its Governor and a host of the Indian Civil Service in the 'Civil Lines' as opposed to the military Cantonment. Our lines were at the far end of cantonments alongside the racecourse, which was one of the main centres of "up country" racing.

Lucknow Residency

Polo was played every Monday, Wednesday and Friday and, on non-polo days each afternoon, I rode out on a young pony into the countryside. I preferred to do so unaccompanied, without a dog or companion to distract my mount. After my orderly, Richbal Singh, had spent six months swinging a polo stick off his back and riding in ever decreasing circles on a loose rein, reining back a stride or two and off again, I took him over and taught him the rest of his polo training during these quiet rides out. The pace was gradually increased, then slowed, all-out dashes followed by quiet walking. My ponies became perfectly balanced and only needed the merest touch of the reins to stop dead from any pace. Then they were put into slow training chukkers, then medium and fast chukkers and finally into tournaments. A period of one and a half years.

We had five polo grounds in Lucknow but these were insufficient for the number of players, and we could often only get six chukkers a day which, for my eight ponies, was a wretched quota. There was some indifferent pig-sticking but quite good shooting on a canal and on certain *jheels* (lakes) in the vicinity, but the polo fraternity had little time to indulge in this sport.

By that time most of India had been electrified, and we had electric light and ceiling fans in place of the old Victorian *punkhas* pulled by a coolie outside on the verandah. This made a tremendous difference to one's comfort, as fans were a far more efficient cooling device and kept going, whereas at intervals during hot weather at night, the *punkha wallah* would go to sleep and one would wake up bathed in sweat. We did not have all that time to rest as it was too hot to go to sleep before midnight, and we were roused at 5 am to go on parade at 6 am. We made up for it by sleeping after lunch until teatime, after which one went out for an evening ride. As the french windows were opened the outside heat hit one in the face like opening the doors of a furnace. My shared bungalow was far from Bombay standards, but was built of brick instead of mud, and far more up to date.

I returned from Bombay with a useful string of ponies. There were many nice people around, but after the fleshpots of Bombay it was high time I engaged myself in soldiering again, more especially as I was shortly due to sit for the exam for promotion to major. The Army officer was pestered with exams; retention exam, promotion to captain, then to major, entry to the staff college if one took it. I suppose that I should have done so but I loved regimental soldiering. It was a trial to sit down and swot up a vast syllabus at the age of thirty. I took a correspondence course, which, to cover itself, embraced every possible aspect of the various subjects; Military Law, Administration, Tactics, History of a campaign, etc. I started one hot weather day when things were dull. All the womenfolk had left for the hill stations, most of the mess were on leave or doing courses, and competitive polo was off. So, instead of the usual siesta after lunch, I sat at my desk and endeavoured to memorise innumerable military manuals. I answered exam papers sent out weekly from London, along with a timetable which had to be kept to. Many were the afternoons when I fell asleep over my desk. Still, it was better to pass the exam than to fail and have to take it, or parts of it, again. The outcome of this was that I passed with the assistance of some useful cribs in the form of dates and references, which no ordinary man could possibly memorise.

In the old days, after their afternoon sport, everyone repaired to the Club, which provided a bar, billiard room, dance hall and various lounges. By the 30's, it became more and more the practice to entertain in one's bungalow. This went for marrieds and bachelors alike. So we started to furnish our rooms with decent furniture which could be made to order, as opposed to having a load of junk supplied by the furniture *wallah*, and which would consist of a bed, two tables, chairs, a dressing table and wardrobe, plus bathroom furniture of tin bath tub, towel rail, and 'thunderbox', the equivalent of a commode. The cost - 10 rupees a month. Everything could be made to order: clothes, footwear, saddlery, curtains, the lot. I had all my polo ponies' bits, made of steel and measured for each individual pony's mouth, made in the regimental Armourer's shop.

Lucknow possessed a remarkably fine native city with many good buildings, remnants of the days of their own Rajas. Its streets, like those of every Indian city, were tortuous and colourful, many of them being given over to a particular trade, be it foodshops, metal workers, cloth vendors and the like.

Perhaps Lucknow's most noteworthy street was that of the brothels, which were reputed to house the most beautiful collection of girls in all India, each expert in entertaining their patrons. I never visited it, but at that time doing so really was not on; the Raj were above such fraternisation, and in any case had one done so, without doubt, one's squadron would have known about it the following day.

Each year we went to Calcutta for their Christmas week, a three day journey for the 24 or so ponies. There was played the Indian Championship polo tournament, and there was also some high class racing on each non-polo day. We could not have afforded to take the ponies all that distance, but for the fact that the Calcutta Turf Club paid the fares. We were the gladiators who provided their Roman holiday. Each winter the Australian shippers brought over some 3,000 animals, their main trade being that of troop horses, the heavier ones for the British Cavalry regiments and the lighter ones for the Indian cavalry. They also brought over several hundred potential polo ponies and show hacks. In the vast Remount Depot each shipper had his appointed area with so many corrals. I knew most of the shippers and walked round examining their wares. If I liked an animal it was vetted and, if sound, shipped up country. I bought three top-class animals each year, of which one would turn out to be a super pony, one high class and the third a not so good, or perhaps it went lame or was ill-tempered.

From 1931 to 1933 my ponies won all the classes for light and middle weight hacks and polo ponies at the Imperial Delhi Horse Show, the biggest and most important show in India. I had a splendid grey which I named Speedway. This pony won the light weight hacks, the middle weight polo ponies and the best trained pony in the show. In all polo classes the two best entrants were lined up with two flags planted some eighty yards distant. On the word "Go" the winner was the first to round the flags and pass the start line. In the Best Trained affair I was up against Richard George of the Central India Horse, an international player and a very fine polo horseman. He was showing a chestnut Indian bred ex-racing pony which I knew was very fast indeed. We lined up for the drama. The judge said:

My best polo pony : 'Speedway'

"Are you ready?"
Long before he said, "Go", Richard and I were half-way up the course. Watching him like a hawk, he was half a length up on us, 20 yards from the flags. I dared not put on the brakes until within 10 yards of my flag, when I clapped them on and Speedway rounded it on his tail. As we set off on the home stretch I saw, out of the corner of my eye, Richard disappearing into the blue. His chestnut did not stop, not in that class anyway and we came in on our own.

I had another memorable win in the Lucknow light weight polo class. Roscoe Harvey (10th Hussars), probably the best horseman in England at that time, had a wonderful pony, who never grew to racehorse size, sired by the famous thoroughbred racehorse Grand Parade. He had won the light weights at Delhi at least once. I had a well-bred Australian pony that I had bought, half-trained, from the Nawab of Bhopal, a 9 handicap player. Roscoe's pony's stud-name was Severn Beach and he called him Sweetie. I was determined to beat him, and called mine Sweeter Still. We were the two finalists and once again round the flags and back. There was nothing between us at the flags, we both turned on a sixpence and mine won by inches. But it was fair to say that Severn Beach lost to a younger animal. Sweeter Still served me marvellously for four seasons of polo, and then suffered a strained hock just before the 1939 war.

These were great triumphs, but when I had won all the available prizes I laid off. I left India with 84 cups; horse shows, polo, golf, etc. and a few years ago it came to me - "Who would want Daddy's cups when I was underground?" So I had them melted down and Jean Walwyn, that ace of equine sculpture, made me a beautiful 9 inch silver foal. A small plaque on the base says:

"This statuette represents the cups and prizes won by Lt. Colonel Denzil Holder and his ponies between 1919 and 1939."
It makes a lovely centrepiece for our dining room table; something that anyone would be glad to own.

* *

At Lucknow, we, in naval terms, lay alongside the 10th Hussars for four years. During this period they learned to play polo, then they out-ponyed and finally outplayed us, and went on to win the coveted 'Inter-Regimental' Tournament, a prize that this famous regiment had won many times prior to 1914.

My regiment, Skinner's Horse, never had more than a two-gun side, that is to say two class players, Will Broadfoot and myself. To win the Indian Cavalry or Inter-Regimental Tournaments you had to have a 4, or at least a 3, gun side, and in the 20's the Indian cavalry fielded three top class teams: the 15th Lancers, the P.A.V.O. and the Central India Horse, all of whom had four gun sides. One or other of them dominated Indian polo for 12 years.

* *

Our regiments were fully trained for war, and we had to keep fit to lead them. When the 1939 war broke out, the cavalry were right on the ball. The Indians, yeoman country folk, were adept at finding the way instinctively across miles of open country. We moved in open formation, and a wave of a flag from the C.O.'s group would alter formation or direction in a matter of seconds. The infantry, on the other hand, were tied down to carefully considered tactics and formations, and from the word 'go' needed some 45 minutes to mount an attack. When in the autumn of 1940 we got to the deserts of the Sudan, our men were in their element. Motorised, as we were then, we would cover five horizons a day, and all we had in the way of maps was a page out of a sixpenny atlas whose scale was about 200 miles to an inch. But we were never at fault in finding the way to our destination. Many of these drives were concluded after dark, but with the brilliant night sky and the light coloured sand, visibility was not too bad.

It was while we were in Lucknow that the terrible Assam earthquake took place. God knows how many people perished. Whole villages were engulfed, roads opened, cars fell into the chasms, the earth's crust closed again, and the cars and their occupants had disappeared. We were some 1,200 miles from the centre of the quake, but one afternoon we were in our bungalows after lunch when strange things started to happen. The bungalow began to shake, pictures rattled and shook on the walls, the light became greenish, and outside the birds squeaked like mad. The penny dropped, as did that of my co-occupant, Douglas Gray. We both nipped, and nipped was the word, into the garden and there we found ourselves in an eerie atmosphere. As we looked from one to the other at a distance of a few yards, he was moving a foot or so to the right and I equally to the left.

"My God!" said Duggie "What the hell is going on?"

"I think it's an earthquake ..."

We felt in the grip of something over which we had no control, out of this world as we knew it. Shortly after, things eased off. The atmosphere cleared to normal, and we returned to our respective quarters, amazed, rather like the shepherds after Bethlehem. Earthquakes are no joke at all. There was another ghastly one in Quetta, which devastated the native city, and much of the widely dispersed cantonments. Houses collapsed like cards and the death toll was enormous.

I think it was that year Douglas Gray from Skinner's Horse won the supreme prize in the pigsticking world, the Kadir Cup, contested by entries from all over India. The Cup took its name from the district in which it was held, miles of flat country some covered by crops but mostly by two to three foot high grass intersected by small steep *nullahs*. A large camp was erected with mess tents, lines for the marrieds and the bachelors, and also for the orderlies and syces alongside the horse lines. Apart from the contestants, many spectators attended. Each day a line of 100 or so beaters were marshalled to arouse the pig population, and the first heat of three riders (spears) followed them. Each heat had an umpire who, when the bearers flushed a rideable (of sufficient age and size) boar, gave the signal to 'Ride', and the heat galloped forward, each intent on getting the first spear (prod) at the pig. The boar was no mean animal; a big one standing as high as a small calf had long curving tusks which were as sharp as a knife blade, which could inflict a terrible wound in a rider's leg or on the legs or flank of his mount. When cornered, the pig would usually charge the nearest horseman. The riders were armed with long bamboo spears, whose heads had been sharpened to a razor edge. Behind was a line of elephants on which those not

The Kadir Bandobast
by Snaffles

competing followed and watched the proceedings.

It took a certain time for the heat to get on terms with the pig, which, considering his bulk was amazingly fast and extremely active. As the heat or the leader of it closed on the pig it would, as often as not, jink left or right in a matter of yards, much quicker than a horse at that speed, and could turn and make off at right angles. Happy then was the spear on that flank who gained some horses' lengths on the next leg. Eventually one of the heat claimed the spear - but had to show blood on it to the umpire to be declared the winner. Pigs, incidentally, did considerable damage to the farmers' crops.

Having attained my Majority (see Frontispiece), I now commanded a squadron in my own right for the first time, as opposed to doing so in the absence of a superior. Since returning from Bombay I had been well brought up by Gerald Gray, now Second-in-Command of the regiment. It gave me a great thrill to ride on to parade towards 120 men and horses lined up with their drawn swords at the slope. As I approached, the Risaldar gave the order:

"'C' Squadron, Carry swords"

at which there was a flash of steel along the two ranks as they brought their swords vertical in front of their right knees. My Second-in-Command reported the parade and I rode round the ranks inspecting each man and his mount. The Indians were very elegant horsemen, slim in leg and bottom, they fitted into their saddles as a hand into a glove. Their cotton drill tunics and breeches were freshly starched and ironed and their *lungis* (turbans) beautifully tied. How proud I was of them - my squadron. These *sowars* (troopers) were the sons of yeomen landowners whose forebears had often served in the regiment for several generations. It was an honour for them to enter Skinner's Horse. How well they served us in the war. They were not fighting for democracy or the British Empire, they served you - personally. What one asked them to do they did, because you asked them. "*Sahib bolta*" (the Sahib says). At the outbreak of the 1939 war the Indian army contained probably the best troops that we had in the Empire. Brave, loyal and "countrywise" intelligent.

During the cold weather most of the big stations had a 'week' during which there was their polo tournament and a race meeting. Lucknow had two such, and each had a fancy dress dance on the final Saturday. Many girls came out from home to spend the winter in India, staying with friends or relations. These girls were sometimes called the "Fishing Fleet", looking for husbands. There were hundreds of young men in India and comparatively few unmarried girls, so their presence was more than welcome. India was a land of tentage; a tent was as big as a room, with double flies to keep out the sun or the cold. Each had its bathroom en suite. With a thick cotton carpet and charcoal heater, they were very luxurious. The furniture *wallah* provided the furniture. The tents were pitched in the hosts' compound, and housed visiting polo players, Steeplechase jockeys, and the girls, each of whom brought their own bearers. When the civil District Officers toured their domains, which could be the size of Wales, they had two 'camps' - the one that they slept in after their day's travel, and the one which they had occupied the night before. This had travelled on ahead of them to be pitched ready to receive them the following night.

In the 'week', the station was full to bursting. The visitors, after a morning ride, had a bath and breakfast, and proceeded on visits or sightseeing until lunch. Horse sports occupied the afternoon, followed by cocktail and dinner parties in the evening.

I took no part in steeplechasing. Many G.R.s (gentlemen riders) took it up as their main sport, but I could not afford to keep chase horses and their training expenses, and I did not wish to risk the chance of crocking myself in a fall.

The last excitement of the week was the Saturday dance. Perhaps we had won the tournament, my ponies had behaved superbly. There was a cocktail party and champagne dinner; lovely music in the magnificient ballroom of the *Chattar Munzil*, (The Golden Umbrella), which had been the riverside palace of the rulers of Oudh, and was now a Club. Around midnight 'we' made our way up on to the roof. The November air was warm and the stars shone as only they can in the East. She was clad in a dark wine velvet frock that only the very slim can wear. She opened her arms and we met and the truth was symbolised, at last, in that first embrace.

"My darling".

"My love".

We stood there, oblivious to all around us, just the strains of the music below. "The touch of God's finger on man's shoulder". There were stars in her eyes and I was in the seventh heaven.

* *

A few weeks after the dance we went with a few friends to visit Benares, the most holy city on the banks of the Ganges. It was there that every Hindu, if he could afford it, wished his corpse to be burnt and his ashes thrown into Mother Ganges. The near bank of the river was lined with scores of temples, most of which, like other Indian temples, were heavily carved, depicting gods and goddesses. One of them was so pornographic that women did not visit it. The morning after our arrival we walked from our hotel in the brilliant cold weather sunshine down to see the sights and the burning ghats. Just short of the river, there, coming towards us was a *fakir*. There were hundreds of them in Benares who lived by alms freely given by the pilgrims and the burial parties to earn merit. This fellow, still dripping with water from his bathe, was almost as broad as he was long, his magnificent torso and limbs matted with hair, his eyes red with drugs, as he stumped towards us completely naked. His testicles would have done credit to a prize bull. Which way to look? How to restart the conversation?

That afternoon I strolled by myself through the narrow alleyways lined with exquisite little shops amongst which was that of a carver in marble, who sat on his shop floor some three feet above the roadway. As I reached him he took a carved figure off the shelf behind him and placed it on the floor for my inspection. It was a nice piece in marble six inches high, of a seated buddha. I asked him *"Kitna?"* (how much); he replied "Ten rupees, Sahib". One always bargained in the East and I told him I would give him eight rupees. He looked at me and replaced the figure on the shelf and went on with his carving. I walked on. Then I thought: "You will regret that figure" and I turned back and bought it. It sits today on our drawing room mantlepiece, quite charming. That same afternoon I visited the "Men only" temple in which the carving was, believe me, an eye opener!

Into the Ganges ran the city drains, and into it were cast the funeral pyre ashes and remnants of hundreds of corpses each day. And each day thousands bathed in the river to purify themselves but, extraordinary to tell, the water was absolutely pure and fit to drink. The Benares waterfront is one of the acknowledged wonders of the world.

We were at Delhi Week together, the year that my grey pony Speedway swept the board in the horse show, and we took two days off to visit Agra and the Taj Mahal, the most beautiful building in the world. It was built by the famous Moghul, Shah Jehan, the grandson of the great Akbar, as a tomb for his Persian wife, Mumtaz Mahal. Shah Jehan scoured the world for craftsmen to fulfil his dream, and the story goes that when the white marble masterpiece was completed he put out the eyes of the Italian architect lest he reproduce its beauty. We went there after dinner, and shimmering under a brilliant moon, there it was, indescribably beautiful and utterly romantic, and we were in love. It was the first time we had been alone together and I shall never forget it.

The Taj Mahal

Delhi Week, like others, held a ball every night, Hog-hunters ball, Fancy dress ball and, the ace and highlight of them all, the Viceroy's Ball. We went together, approaching the vast Viceroy's House up Kingsway. At night, it was lit by rows of lamps and, half way up the drive and bridging it, stood the immense red sandstone war memorial. Its top was shaped into a flat crucible twenty feet across in which, during the week, was burnt some substance which gave off a blue smoke by day and smouldering red flame by night. Overhead, stars shone like diamonds in the clear black sky. Troopers of the Viceroy's Bodyguard in gold lace turbans and scarlet tunics, white breeches and long top boots, lined the steps, each with a tall lance with a red and white pennant. The palace was a blaze of lights. A.D.C.s received a thousand guests, and shephered them towards the cloakrooms. The ballroom was thronged with every mess kit in the Army, civilians in tail coats wearing their orders, every woman in her very best frock. Dozens of Indian Princes were present, wearing knee length coats of silk and satin, white, blue, yellow and green, with turbans and jewels such as you have never seen. Ropes of pearls down to their waists, diamonds, emeralds, sapphires. It was unbelievable. The ball presented a spectacle which will never be seen again and in what a setting! How privileged one was to have been there. The Raj in all its social glory.

* * * * *

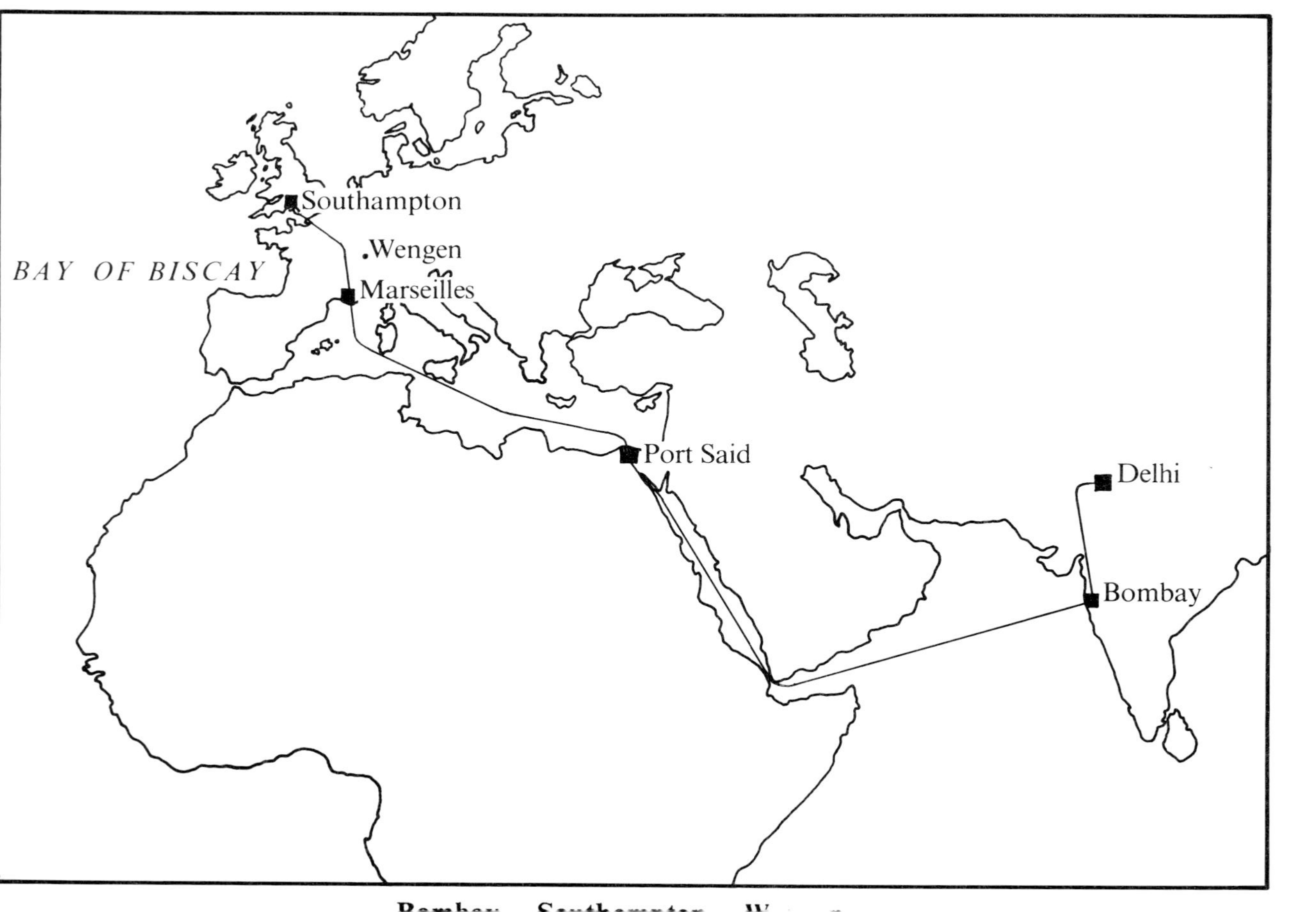
Southampton
.Wengen
BAY OF BISCAY
Marseilles
Port Said
Delhi
Bombay

CHAPTER IX

MY LEAVES

Apart from two months' leave every year, long leaves, known in the old days as furlough, came up every three years or so, when one was entitled to a year's leave. Furlough in bygone days was quite a business, entailing furnishing a cabin and sailing in a sailing ship round the Cape. With the opening of the Suez Canal and the advent of steam ships, things became easier and the taking of leave more general.

In my day the voyage took three weeks by P & O from Bombay to Tilbury, though the journey could be shortened by travelling overland from Marseilles - thereby cutting out six days via the Bay of Biscay. Joining in 1918, I took my first leave in 1924. Prior to that I was happy enough in India and did not want to sell my polo ponies to defray the cost of the return trip which was a matter of £120.

In those days, when motor cars were few and far between, the 'up country' newspapers, the "Pioneer" and the "Civil & Military Gazette", contained three pages of "Horses for Sale" and one could glean the circumstances of one's friends from these advertisements. Times changed and after the outbreak of the 1939 war there would not have been more than half a column.

I applied, and was granted, a passage on a troop ship which was much cheaper than sailing by one of the commercial lines, but entailed doing duties as required by the ship's adjutant, and wearing uniform in the evening. I did orderly officer in the Bay of Biscay, when one of the duties was the inspection of the troops' mess decks. This was not very pleasant, as half the troops aboard were desperately sick and the stench was quite appalling. One felt frightfully sorry for them and I did not feel too well myself.

We landed at Southampton on the 23rd December and, wanting to go to my home in Somerset, I was detailed to take a draft to York, of all places. My draft of 20 soldiers and I arrived at York at 7.0 pm after a long journey and I thought that the regiment, whose men I had escorted, would invite me to spend the night with them in their mess. Not so. A sergeant met the train, checked and signed for the draft, saluted and left me standing on the platform. Some hours later I got a slow train to London where I arrived at 7 am tired, dirty and unshaven and it was an hour before the first taxi appeared. I asked the driver where he thought I could get in to a hotel.

"Gor lummy, Sir, on Christmas Eve, you 'aven't a 'ope."
But he took me to the Strand Palace Hotel, who allowed me to clean up and do a change in their vast 'gents'. From there I set out for my tailor. How different the 1924 London was from that which I had last seen in 1918 - when it was crammed with uniforms from all over the Empire, Canadians, New Zealanders, dashing Flying Corps officers and most spectacular of all, the occasional Indian Cavalry officer with his long *kurta* (tunic) and chains on his shoulders. Now it seemed humdrum, no troops, no uniforms, only rather shabby civilians. I was a soldier. I squared my shoulders and walked out. I passed a newsvendor, who looked at me and exclaimed:

"Naw then Mister - don't yer know the war's over."
I could have murdered him! I arrived home late on Christmas Eve.

In January some friends asked my younger sister and me to go ski-ing in Wengen, a stronghold of the English. In fact, who in those days skied except the English? I took to it easily, and loved it. In 1924 skis were prehistoric horrors, and I wore riding breeches, puttees and old boots. This holiday led to my meeting a very delightful woman, elegant, witty and very much "with it". We became lovers and back in London laughed and danced to all hours at the famous Quadrant, haunt of the Prince of Wales; and also at the Florida and the Ambassadors - night clubs which were all the rage in those days. In the mornings we would walk in Bond Street, where the rank and fashion were to be seen, beautifully dressed, jewelled and scented. I lived in London in a whirl of love, glamour and excitement. My home I found dull; my father and mother had parted, there was little money and my mother and my five brothers and sisters led a very small-town existence. I had sold three of my ponies and was in funds. Friends gave me some hunting and fishing but London was - well, London.

My next leave was in 1927. That winter I had joined the Governor's Bodyguard in Bombay, and being due for furlough, they allowed me four months' leave before the 'season' started in Poona. This leave followed much the same pattern as that in 1924. I bought myself a black and white two-seater sports car of which I was very proud. It had an enormous exhaust pipe and emitted an exciting deep-throated roar.

I did well and got leave again in 1929. A friend of mine, John Nethersole, who had previously commanded the Bombay Bodyguard, asked me if I would like to go to Budapest and run the Hungarian Polo Club for their polo season. Having been there the previous season, he painted a glamorous picture of their wonderful ponies, super women and the gipsy music. I went. I was put up by the Club in the Duna Palota (Ritz) hotel on the banks of the Danube. What a city! Old Buda on one side of the river with its palaces and villas, and Pest on the other side with its commerce, superb shops and hotels - surely one of the most beautiful cities in the world, if only for its hauntingly exciting gipsy music and its beautiful bridges over the river, joining the old and new towns together. My time there was a highlight in my life. I lived '*en prince*'.

The Hungarians have a very special charm, as have their neighbours in Austria. They had a tremendous love of all field sports, their particular one being "the shootings", and their bags of pheasants paled those of the best English shoots into insignificance. Their women had immense personal charm. Their horses - it has been said that the ordinary Hungarian farmer knew as much about horse breeding as did all but the most expert of our blookstock industry. In the Middle Ages the continental armies mounted their cavalry largely on Hungarian horses. These horses were extraordinarily amenable; so much so that the young Hungarians, if they saw a likely looking animal in a cart, would have it sent round to

NORTH SEA
BALTIC SEA
London
Amsterdam
Berlin
Frankfurt
Vienna
Strasburg
Paris
Munich
Budapest
Zurich
Venice
Lyon
Milan
Florence
ADRIATIC SEA
Marseilles
Rome
MEDITERRANEAN

their stable, and saddle it the next day. The country carts were often pulled by four-in-hand, the leaders harnessed by a head collar attached by ropes to the cart.

The Polo Club was run by Bolvin, Duke of Mecklenburg, who was a nephew of the Kaiser, and had been cashiered from a crack cavalry regiment owing to some scandal over a woman. He left Germany and went to the Argentine where he worked as a stock rider. When the 1914 war broke out he found his way back to Germany as a stoker on a tramp steamer. He ended the war as a Brigadier defending Berlin against the communist mobs. Bolvin was a typical Junker, autocratic, bombastic, a great disciplinarian and sportsman. After the war, and again reinstated, he married a beautiful circus girl and was once more driven out of society. His wife took the title of princess, which infuriated the Hungarian nobility, who were mostly countesses. They hated the Germans anyway.

Bolvin got his job when Hungary was impoverished after the 1918 war, when he pointed out to the government that one of their assets were their horses, and that polo would provide a shop window for them. He was installed in the Duna Polata in a fine suite of rooms with a small salary. He had no money, as, following the scandal, he had been cut off by his family.

Polo did not 'go' with the Hungarian aristocracy, apart from Counts Wenckheim and Karoly. The President's son, Pista Betlen, played, as did both sons of the Regent, Admiral Horthy. These two families were very important to the Duke and to his job, and I quarrelled with him as he always allotted the best of the 40 Club ponies to these three men, to the detriment of other players.

I motored out to Hungary at the beginning of May in a 2-seater model Ford. Getting on the road at 6 a.m. it was a lovely trip through France, crossing the Rhine at Strasbourg, through Bavaria where the untarred roads were lined with primroses and bluebells, through Vienna and down the Danube to Budapest. Polo was just starting. I was given four good ponies which proved easy to get on with, and like most of the ponies, had beautiful mouths. In June, Count Wenckheim took a team over to Vienna to play in the Austrian

European championship; we were a good team, the weak link as ever, being the patron. I was put up in style in the famous Bristol Hotel, made a member of their Jockey Club, and initiated to Zachars, the restaurant of the aristocracy.

The Mecklenburgs gave me a lift to Vienna in a 12-cylinder Sunbeam sports car. He had wangled the agency from Sunbeams and this car was given to him as the shop window for the make. The Mecklenburgs were in front and I sat behind on a diminutive seat, from which I was lucky on several occasions not to be decanted, as we went over a bad bump in the road. As we neared the Austrian frontier, a furious altercation took place between the Duke and his wife. Their passports? He had them. No, she had them. The upshot of this was that we had to return to the Hotel, where they had been left. This made us very late indeed, and it was dark long before we arrived at the frontier. At 3 am there was some indecision as to whether we had lost our way, but a house came up with all its lights ablaze. Bolvin got out to enquire and, on returning, said something to the Princess at which they both laughed but would not tell me why. Later he explained that it was a high-class brothel run for the benefit of the officers of the Vienna Garrison.

We finally arrived at the Bristol at 5 am. Vienna, a beautiful sight in the early morning light ... "Vienna, city of my dreams"! sang Richard Tauber.

There were six teams entered for the tournament, all of which were promoted by wealthy patrons. Arriving on the ground for the first round's play, Denise Wenckheim looked at the programme and the teams and exclaimed:

"Phuie ... a Jew. Again a Jew."

"But Denise, if there were no Jews, there would be no polo," I said quietly. In fact one of them was Louis Rothschild, the head of the Austrian banking consortium, who was a great friend of theirs and a very nice man indeed. Generally speaking, the Jew was anathema to the Hungarians.

We won the tournament, beating Prince (George) Fugger's team in the final, and a very tough game it was.

There were super parties given while we were there. The first was given by Baron Franzi Mayer-Melnhof on a Danube steamer which he had chartered for the occasion. Its top deck, in total darkness, was reserved for love-making, that below was jazz saxophones, gilt chairs and brilliantly lit; and below that was all greenery, soft lights and a gypsy string band. We went aboard at 11 pm after dining - we never dined before 9 pm - and sailed up river. Very romantic it was with the lights of the city and the swish of our passage. About 1 am the boat slowed to the speed of the current and a searchlight played on the bank, where a bevy of damsels danced for us in diaphanous garments. When the act was finished, the girls withdrew and in the darkness proceeded to change their rig - until the searchlight was switched on to them. There they were, amid shrieks, mostly naked. Prolonged applause from the spectators.

The second party was given by Louis Rothschild in his palace. We drove up a long approach, lined every 20 yards by men in the Rothschild livery, each carrying a pole with a lighted torch attached to it. Inside, the palace was a blaze of chandeliers and magnificient furnishings, and the pick of Austrian society. In the splendid ballroom a superb gypsy orchestra played for us. We were handed 'Paul Poiret' glasses which had no bottoms, only a glass ball, so the glasses could not be put down until their contents had been emptied. The contents, of course, were champagne, poured out of large silver beakers by powdered footmen. It was a ball to remember and we, the winning team and the heroes of the hour, had our pick of the beautiful ladies to dance with.

Then it was our turn for the Hungarian European Championship, in which most of the European teams contested with the addition of a team out from England. We won our opening rounds, and were faced with the Rothschild team in the final. On the night previous to this the Wenckheims gave a ball, which was to be one of the highlights of the season. Champagne flowed as usual, and, as usual, it was a splendid occasion.

After the season ended I spent a happy fortnight with the Wenckheims at their castle O'Kigos, near the Rumanian border. I was taken out to the Hortobarghy, the great plain famous for its wildfowl shooting and for herds of semi-wild horses. In the winter one could shoot duck there until the barrels of one's guns were too hot to hold. The horses were herded by *chikos* - horsemen who lived out on the plain throughout the year, including the bitter cold of the winter, when even the fast-flowing Danube froze over.

Before leaving Buda I had promised to play for Louis Rothschild in a tournament to be held at Frankfurt-on-Main in Germany later in the month. I set out from O'Kigos to motor back across Europe. The tournament was to be held by Baron Carl von Weinberg, the aniline-dye king of Germany. He was the counterpart of our Lord Lonsdale and, like him, a breeder of thoroughbreds and one of the biggest and most successful owners on the turf. He lived in a magnificent domain, Waldfried Castle. As I left Vienna it got hotter and hotter, and I was reduced to a pair of thin drill trousers, no socks and a shirt open to the waist - like the hot weather in India. I never realised how hot central Europe could be in the summer. On the evening of the third day I was in Karlsruhe and out of cigarettes so I entered a tobacconist and stuttered out "Haben sie cigaretten Englander?". The shop owner quizzed me and said:

"I suppose what you want is a tin of Goldflake, no?"

He added:

"Why spend the night in the heat of the town? Better to go up to Herrenalp, it is only twenty kilometres in the Black Forest. I have a nephew there who keeps a Gasthaus. If you like I will phone him and book you a room."

I was very grateful to him for his kind suggestion and the cool night in that delightful little resort. On again next day, a Sunday, along the Rhine and, twenty miles short of Frankfurt, I had a puncture - my only trouble of the trip. I changed the wheel, and covered in dust, I arrived at Walfried Castle. As I drew up, the portals opened and a posse of footmen positioned themselves down a flight of steps and, between them, a butler slowly descended. Behind him appeared a film- star-looking young man.

"Captain Holder? Come in."

I was, I said, filthy, and demurred.

"Don't worry about that", he said. "What you want is a whisky and soda and a bath. Come in and I will mix you a drink."

I entered a magnificent hall and, while I waited, I saw, laid out on a long table, rows of English, German and French weeklies and dailies. Heading the English pile was the "Express" with the heading:

"Terrible heat-wave persists over Europe".

This was the answer to my last four days of travel.

As the castle could not house all the fifty or sixty guests, some went to villas of friends. I was taken to mine which I was to share with the Wenckheims. In its beautifully furnished drawing room I picked up a German weekly, "Die Damen". An article pictured an elegant villa, its frontage, its grounds and swimming pool and an interior featuring a Chinese tapestry over the mantlepiece. I thought the tapestry seemed familiar and looking up, there it was. The article concerned the villa in which I was staying. Every night there was dancing. The best gypsy band from Hungary had been engaged to play, and a bonga-bonga band brought over from the Argentine to provide a contrast. At intervals a spotlight picked out a couple and they were presented with costly prizes - pearls, gold handbags, fitted suitcases. One night Charles Gairdner (10th Hussars) and I were sitting with the Baron and, emboldened with wine, one of us asked him

"Baron, if it is not a rude question, what does this party cost a day?"

The old man considered.

"Let me see. In your monies, say £1,000 to £1,200." (That would be £5,000 to £6,000 to-day!) He continued:

"I do not spend my monies on gambling or ze womans, only for sport, and I like to see you young men and your polo."

The week was spoilt by heavy thunderstorms following the great heat, and we never finished the tournament. We had one extra game in which the Baron was to play (he was over 80 but still in good trim) and his side had to win, and win he did, but only by one of our side skilfully putting the ball through our own goal - this amid derisive cheers by all the players.

Louis Rothschild had a well-known character as his 'master of horse', one Jimmy Pearce, who had served in the British cavalry. Towards the end of the week he asked me if

Cartoon of Baron Franze Mayer-Melnhof, Vienna.

I would come out again and play in the Rothschild team at a house-party polo tournament to be given by the Mayer-Melnhofs at his chateau in the Semmering. I told Jimmy that I was satiated with beautiful women, champagne and living it up, and all I wished to do was to take my rod to some quiet English trout stream and fish.

"Fish", he said, "If you want fishing the Semmering has some of the best in Europe."

I was hooked.

A fortnight or so later I received from the Rothschild's London agent a first-class ticket on the Blue Train to Vienna, and a cabin on the cross-Channel boat. Being a 'hired assassin' had its points! Jimmy had inveigled me to go out a few days before polo started to help him school the team ponies. In the evenings I was taken out to various streams to fish, and very productive they were, lovely little trout of about half a pound, beautifully marked with brilliant crimson, yellow, blue and black spots. I was attended by a small boy dressed in semi-rags but sporting a battered black Austrian hat with a long feather perched behind it. He carried over his shoulder a canister filled with water, into which one's catch was slipped and the fish kept alive for the pot. On arrival back at the chateau I tipped the catch into a large horse trough behind the house and told my hostess of their number. Somewhat to my chagrin she said that this was nice but actually all the requirements as regards food were on order from Vienna and delivered daily. On inspection of the trout she said that they were very small, and she knew a place where there were fish five times that size. It was arranged that we went there the next day. The Mayer-Melnhof family had started life in a stone-walled arrow-slotted keep on the top of a nearby mountain. As things quietened down they moved to a small castle, also on a hill top. Later again they descended to a moated grange, still with battlements, and finally lived in the chateau alongside the river. All these structures she pointed out to me, and it was to the moated grange that we were to go and fish. On arrival one could see in the moat water some whopping big trout and, stretching a line, I had, within half an hour, three of them between 3 and

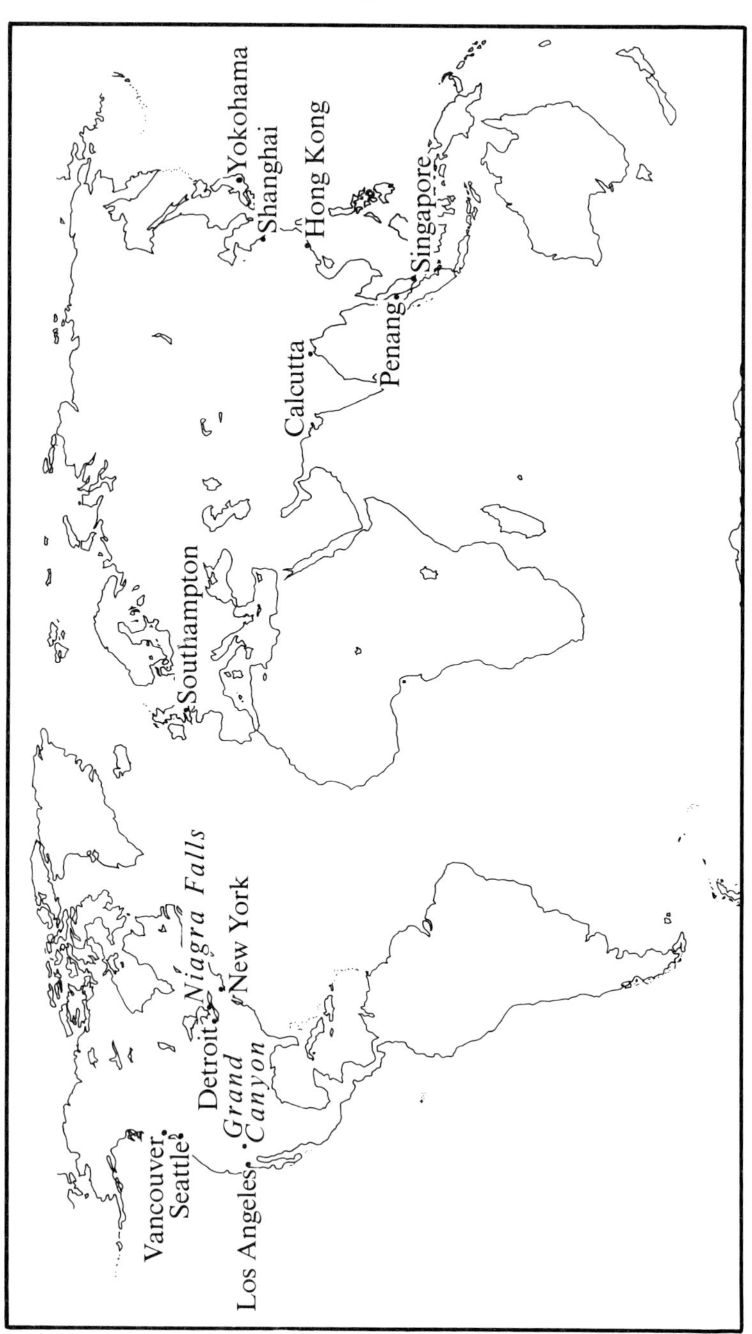

Around the World

4 lbs. Marie was clapping her hands with delight when she spied one of their *jaegers* leaning over a fence and watching the proceedings,

"See, Hans, how the Major catches our trout?"

"Yes," he replied "All of them are breeding trout."

I was fishing their hatchery!

Marie had a charming lot of guests, who played polo, tennis, flirted, and danced in glorious weather. A shoot was laid on when deer and chamois were blanked in from a huge area of forest, and skilfully directed through the line of guns. We took up our allotted positions and, shortly afterwards, stags came crashing through the undergrowth. I shot a stag and for me that was enough. Three little chamois came forward and stopped to crop grass nervously only a few yards away; a beautiful sight - why kill them? I never knew that chamois were to be found in the forest, imagining them only on rocky alpine heights.

1931 was for me was a year of triumph and glory but, finally, disaster.

I was having a great time in these years. I was at the height of my polo career, I had some first-class ponies, I had plenty of money in my pocket, largely through the sale of my ponies. Further to the point, having had leave in 1929, I got another eight months in 1931. I engaged to travel home with a few friends 'the other way round' that is, via Burma, Hong Kong, Japan and America. After the Inter-Regimental polo tournament, we set off to Calcutta. Those who had served on Government House staffs always had the entree to other A.D.C. rooms. I was invited to meet Douglas Fairbanks, who was staying there for a few days before doing a shooting trip. Fairbanks arrived with his golf pro and a P.A. He had been playing golf at Tollygunge, one of the Calcutta courses. He was a small man, but with a superb athletic figure, the brightest of grey eyes, and tremendous personality. One of the A.D.C.s said:

"Can I introduce Major Holder - he is on his way to Hollywood".

"Hollywood!" said Fairbanks. "Here, cable my brother Robert, 'Major Holder arrives soon, will you look after him?'"

We sailed two days' later, and spent two nights in the little port of Penang. There we saw that the water below our restaurant was alive, with phosphorescent, gleaming sea snakes. Horrible! Penang was a lovely little place but like all eastern ports from Aden to Shanghai very muggy. In Singapore friends took us to their clubs. Hong Kong, still not over-built, was a delight, the harbour a wonderful sight at night. There we bought silks and curios in the markets. On to Shanghai, and that was the crux of the trip. I left the other two, and while they waited for the arrival of two more of their regiment, I left ahead for Japan. We had meant to go up to Peking but, what with expenses at the various ports of call, and with America ahead, we had cut it out. A great pity, as we would have seen it in the 'Ginger Griffin' days before the revolution.

Japan was in 'blossom time', the peak of its attraction, but I was in no mood to appreciate it, and marred by my kit being 'gone through' by, presumably, the police, and also by the beggars who swarmed round the tourist spots, many of them being horribly disfigured.

I sailed from Yokohama and, as I was walking down to the quay, I was importuned by a shop-keeper to buy pyjamas from silk material that he displayed on his arm. I said:

"No good to me, I am sailing this afternoon."

He enquired, "What time and what ship?"

I said, "The X Maru, 14.30."

"OK, mister. You choose silk, price 8 yen, I have them aboard before you sail. You pay me on ship."

I chose three of his gorgeous silks and walked on. The time was just short of mid-day. A few minutes before the gangway was due to be raised, up rushed a little Jap with a big cardboard box. He approached me,

"Your pyjamas, Sir."

Being wary of the Japs I opened the box to check that it did indeed contain three suits of pyjamas and not newspaper but there they were, beautifully made and still hot from the iron. No wonder the Japs have made their markets. The suits lasted me for ten years, and could not have been bettered in Jermyn Street.

It was the end of April and on the N.W. passage to Vancouver it was very cold and very rough. Vancouver was delightful. I did a motor trip round the island with an old American and his wife who were very, very 'Boston' and very charming. I crossed over to Seattle and was then in the States. From there I took a train down the West coast to Los Angeles where, having wired my time of arrival, I was met by a vast Cadillac complete with Jap chauffeur sent by United Artists. I was put up at a grand hotel as a guest of the studio, and woke next morning to the phone ringing. A woman's voice enquired,

"Is that Major Holder?"

"Yes," I said.

"Well, Major, we have been waiting for your arrival in Hollywood, and we very much want your picture for one of our top papers. Would you be so kind as to step into the studio of 'Melbourne Spur' which adjoins the hotel foyer, who will take the picture?"

Flattered beyond belief, the fabulous Hollywood wanting Holder's photo, I went along after breakfast and presented myself. Waiting while a film star was being dealt with I looked at several portrait albums in the foyer and I have never seen the like. The whole business of my attending was a simple advertising stunt to get me to buy some of the shots, which indeed I did. I did not come out 'as a God' but they were very high class productions. Next door to 'Melbourne Spur' was a drug store which I entered to buy some cigarettes. There in the shop was a fellow looking exactly like my idea of John the Baptist. He was dressed in a rough white robe tied at the waist with a length of rope. Long white locks fell on his shoulders and he held two greyhounds on a leash. I nudged the person next to me and asked who the guy was,

"Say, don't you know him? That's Peter the Hermit."

This character lived in a cave somewhere up in Beverley Hills, where he sold love-potions and told fortunes. In Hollywood one dressed the part.

1931 was the year of depression, world depression, and it hit the film industry like every other business. In India it cut our pay by 10%. And the studios cut back on their productions. It was the ambition of good looking girls in the States to become film stars and by hook or by crook they graduated to

D.H. in Hollywood

Hollywood to catch the eye of someone in films who, they hoped, would get them into films and maybe to stardom. The streets of the film world teemed with beautiful, really beautiful girls who would stop at nothing to get a few dollars to spend on their keep and their make-up, and to continue their quest for employment. I was taken to various parties and met quite a few of world-renowned stars. I thought, generally speaking, they fell a lot short of their image that I had seen on the screen and were not to be compared, in looks, with the aspirants to fame. But some of them had tremendous charm.

The day after I arrived I went along to United Artists, which was almost a small town in itself with its offices, quarters, sets for various types of films or scenes, and asked for one of Fairbanks' managers, whom I will call Blake. The guard at the entrance allowed me in, and I was taken along to Blake's office. He was a most delightful chap, sincere, efficient and very charming, the very best type of American. He asked me what I wanted to see in Hollywood.

"Well," I said, "What about Clara Bow?"

Clara Bow was the original 'It girl', 'Sex kitten' or what have you. The male population was mad about her. Blake ruminated,

"Clara Bow", he said. "No - not that one."

Somewhat abashed I then suggested seeing round the studio.

"That's nothing more than a machine shop. I will take you out to the Country Club."

This was one of the top golf courses, laid out regardless of cost and very different from our home courses with their narrow, heather-bordered fairways. The Americans go out to play golf, not to mess about looking for lost balls. So their fairways at the tee are all of a hundred yards in breadth to some eighty yards short of the green. The only thing to be said for the average British course is the low cost of membership and green fees.

Blake arranged for me to attend one of their fabulous first nights at the Sid Grauman Chinese theatre, and for me to stand next to the boss as he greeted the arriving stars under the floodlights. The loud speaker announced:

"Miss So-and-So and Mr. X."

Miss So-and-So flashed her best smile for rows of movie cameras, kissed or shook hands with Grauman, and passed in. It was a privileged experience for an outsider.

I had a letter of introduction to Stewart Iglehart who played No.3 for the American international team. He took me to the Los Angeles Stock Exchange and explained the financial slump which was ruining thousands of businesses throughout the States. The room which we entered was as long as a hanger and, hung on the wall down the entire length, were a series of blackboards, each of which represented a particular stock and the current price.

"Come over here", said Iglehart.

"Here is American Steel, which is one of the backbones of the American economy."

Alongside each board was a man on a ladder wearing earphones who corrected the prices on the board as they came in over the phone. As I watched he rubbed out and chalked in the fall in price .. 89, 88.70, 88.30 and so on. Said Iglehart:

"There are our fortunes, dwindling every hour."

I felt that I was lucky to be on a salary even if it had been cut by 10%.

When I was due to leave Hollywood, Blake sent me a suitcase containing 12 bottles of whisky (100% proof) and warned me not to touch any other spirits. On enquiry he told me that, with prohibition in force, illicit stills were working all over the country making 'moonshine' - unmatured spirit made from potatoes which could be poison. He told me how, only a week before, one of their salesmen had met his opposite number in a small town in the Middle-West. They had told the bell-hop (page boy) to bring a bottle of whisky to their room. Needless to say they finished the bottle, and their man had been found in bed the next morning green and stiff. Hootch!

How kind they were to me. I went along to the travel bureau in the hotel to book my ticket onward, which included the Grand Canyon, the wheat and oil country of the Middle West, Detroit, where I wanted to see the Ford factory and its first in the world automatic car assembly line. Then Niagara Falls: "The highlight of your tour, Major", and down the Hudson river to New York. The ticket was some three feet long and comprised perforated sections which were torn off it at various stages. It dealt with four days' travel, and cost quite a bit in sterling. The dollar bought much the same as a shilling but there were only $2.50 to the pound.

That was the end to the most glamorous place in the world at that time. How much did we enjoy it? I boarded the train and, after an hour or so, was in the Californian desert and terribly hot it was. Early the next morning I left the train at the Grand Canyon station, to spend the day there. The canyon is the most wonderful sight. A tremendous rift in the earth's surface some three miles across, and dropping down, the Colorado river was visible as a tiny silver thread some thousands of feet below. The sides of the rift are a mass of brilliant colours, red, yellow, green and gold - an amazing sight.

On again through the wheat belt for two days, with oil derricks sprouting on both sides of the line, and very dull it was. I could not afford a drawing-room and travelled in a 'day car', and had a sleeping berth in a carriage next door. We stopped for meals in wayside station restaurants, as in India. The sleeping berths were just curtained off bunks for both sexes along each side of the carriage and, once in, one had to perform gymnastic feats to dress and undress in them. The carriage was shut at 7.30 pm which was far too early to go sleep and the only place to go was the men's washroom at one end. My co-travellers were Americans sitting around in their shirt-sleeves, smoking ghastly cigars and at frequent intervals spitting - usually with unerring accuracy - into a row of spitoons in the centre of the floor. What a journey! On day three we arrived at Detroit, and there I took a bus tour round the Ford works, and very interesting it was.

From there to Niagara Falls, the Brighton and Southend for American honeymoon couples. I stood at the bottom of the gigantic falls. This was one of the wonders of the world but I had seen it pictured in my first school atlas, and numerous representations of it ever since. Was I in a somewhat sour frame of mind? I was! I took another bus tour, where we were shown an enormous rubber ball inside which some lunatic went over the Falls and, unlike others, had survived. While we looked another lunatic went over the Falls in a barrel. We followed it as it dashed down the cataract below the Falls and entered the whirlpool further downstream. There it circled round and round and, after a bit, a flag appeared out of an opening signalling for help; the barrel had sprung a leak. A motor boat went out and the barrel and its occupant were towed ashore.

On arrival in New York I stayed very much down-town in 26th street. The hotel was not expensive but the meals were, so I had recourse to a lunch counter across the street where they produced splendid snacks (a word still unknown in England) and excellent coffee. In 1931 prohibition was at its height; hootch runners, hi-jackers and gangsters abounded and gang battles with sub-machine guns were the order of the day. A coal merchant tipped a load of coal into the street and everyone within earshot flung themselves flat thinking that it was a burst of automatic fire. I was taken to various 'speakeasies'.

I had a letter of introduction to Devereux Milburn, who had captained the American polo team. Oxford educated, he married an English girl and they were very much top society in Meadowbrook, Long Island, the home of American polo. Milburn had very kindly arranged for me to be an honorary member of the Racquets Club, which was one of their top clubs, and invited me to spend a week-end at their home. I met him at his office in Wall Street which was situated on the 30-something floor. The lift sped upward at incredible speed. Milburn greeted me with:

"You must be surprised to see me here as I retired years ago. But here I am again, trying to salve the remains of my fortune."

He drove me over the magnificent East River bridge to his lovely home, an hour's run from the city. That night at dinner his butler leant over my shoulder and whispered:

"Red wine, white wine, whisky or beer Sir?"

I turned to Mrs. Milburn and asked her:

"How come?"

She replied that they had their own bootlegger, and to rest assured that every bottle in the house had been individually laboratory tested.

The following day, Saturday, they took me to the Meadowbrook Club, where I watched the fabulous Tommy Hitchcock playing. He was a marvellous striker of the ball but a cruel horseman. Immensely powerful in leg and arm, his ponies had to 'go' and 'stop', and I was told that his mounts seldom lasted him for more than one season. The next day we all went over to lunch with a famous sporting character, Ambrose Clarke, where some 20 horse-sport notables were gathered. We talked horses, while drinking American martinis, for two hours or so, and finally sat down to a sumptuous lunch.

After this I stayed with friends in Park Avenue, New York's Park Lane. We dined at the famous La Riche roof restaurant, arriving in the lift with the chauffeur carrying eight bottles of wine and liqueurs all wrapped in brown paper. These were taken over by the doorman at the top, and appeared later on our table. The restaurant could not be accused of selling liquor, and in any case they had come to terms with the cops in regard to this procedure.

I had decided to buy a second-hand American automobile, having heard that they could be bought for a song. This was not the case, and to buy a new one, albeit of a lesser quality, I went along to the General Motors block where there were separate shops for each of their makes: Buick, Oldsmobile etc. and a separate block for Chevrolets. As I got inside the door, the doorman called out:

"Brown."

A man at the end of a long bench came forward.

What did I want? A convertible? "Here is the model you require." Its colour was green with a yellow line. I wanted a black one with a red line. That was difficult, as the green colour was being produced for the current fortnight, and the black ones not for another ten days. I was sailing for home in four days' time. Brown and I got talking. Where was I from? I said from India.

"Say, you are from Hindu land?"

Well, we would have lunch together, and afterwards go to the G.M. block offices, where Brown had a contact with one of the bosses. We whizzed up to the top of the building, where he scribbled something on a card. This gained us entry to a large and sumptuous office. A handsome and elegant man rose from sumptuous office where a very handsome and elegant man rose from his desk and shook my hand.

"This is Major Holder from Hindu land. He wants ..."

Van Ingen, for that was his name, said that he would see what he could do. He phoned the docks; had they a black Chev body? They had.

"Hold it and I will ring you back."

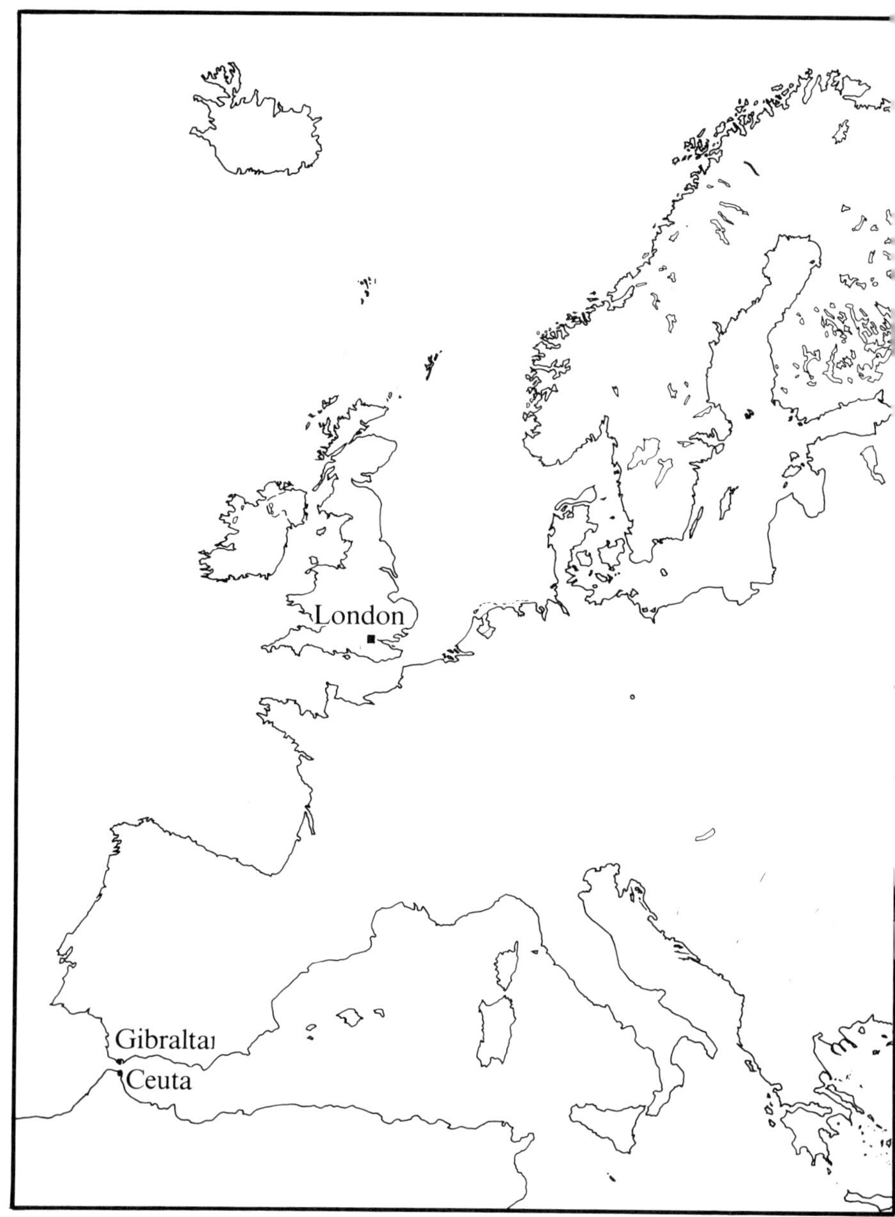

India - Gibraltar - London

Then on to the factory at Detroit; had they a right hand drive chassis? They had. Van Ingen smiled and said that the assembled car would be aboard my ship. I thanked him. General Motors were selling hundreds of Chevs a day, and this top executive had gone to all this trouble to accommodate a single visitor to their country. When I entered my cabin on the ship there was a splendid bouquet of flowers and a bottle of champagne. I thought someone has made a mistake, but not so. I looked at the attached card and it read: "Major Holder - with compliments of General Motors". America at her best; one can see how and why they have such success in business.

The White Star liner was one of the largest of Cunard's fleet, but I did not enjoy the voyage. I was alone once more. Arriving at Southampton there was a train waiting. It looked like a toy compared with the double-size American trains. There was a whistle and almost in silence it pulled out of the station. I was home.

My next leave home was in 1934. I had an invitation to stay with General 'Tim' Harrington, at that time the Governor of Gibraltar. I had arranged in India to have a green two-seater Chrysler convertible to meet me in Gib, and had planned a wonderful tour through Spain to include attending the Easter midnight mass at Seville cathedral, a visit to the Alcazar, and then a stay with Prince Max and Perdita Hohenlohe at their castle outside Madrid. I had met them in Budapest in 1929.

As my ship anchored off Gib, an A.D.C. came out in a launch and took me to the harbour and on to The Convent - an odd name for Government House. The Fleet Air Arm had been executing manoeuvres in the Western Mediterranean and, prior to their departure for home waters, the Rock Admiral had laid on a dance for some of the fleet officers at Admiralty House. About 8 pm a storm had blown up; so fierce was it that it was impossible for the selected officers to come ashore. We had had dinner, in dinner jackets, when the phone rang from Admiralty House. They explained their predicament in regard to partners and asked if the Governor's staff would help them out. His Excellency, informed at once, said that of course everyone would go to their assistance, and told us to hurry up and get into tail coats and be round there in fifteen minutes. We were replete with an excellent meal, coffee, brandy and cigars, and getting down to a quiet chat before going off to bed. But off we went to our rooms, dug out our clothes and were propelled off to the dance.

We were met by a Naval A.D.C. who guided us to the bar, where a Petty Officer in charge poured each of us a tumbler of the strongest Martini I had ever tasted. The dance ended at 4 am. We were not woken until 11. We had done our stuff by the Royal Navy.

Next morning I received a cable from Chryslers in America which read:

"Regret that owing to strike cannot deliver your car before June."

My whole trip was ruined and I learned from the shipping office that all the immediate boats to England were fully booked. I was telling this to the Military Secretary when His Excellency himself came into the office. Rosie Weir explained.

"Well", said the General, "he had better go home with the Fleet. I am sure that Ramsey will take him. I will ask him at lunch."

And to me:

"You had better get your things packed."

Admiral Ramsey and his immediate staff were due to arrive in half an hour, and I dashed upstairs and crammed my belongings into their cases. The Admiral kindly agreed. During lunch the storm blew up again. The meal over, and goodbyes completed, we drove down to the waterfront to board a little paddle boat which was to take us out to the Flagship, the aircraft carrier Courageous. All went well inside the harbour, but once we were out of it we met the full force of the gale and were in trouble. One moment we were 100 yards from the towering bulk of the carrier, and the next moment we were in dire danger of ramming her. Her captain shouted through a megaphone:

"You can't come aboard, Sir."

He was the ship's captain and the Admiral had no choice, but Hell broke loose, everyone damned everyone else but to no effect and we trundled back into the shelter of the harbour, and there our party boarded one of the two escort destroyers.

The plan was to move over to Algeciras where there should be sufficient lee to effect the transfer to the carrier. The gale increased to typhoon strength, and the air indicator showed 130 mph and beyond it. So plan 2 was to cross the straits to Ceuta. While the bosses occupied the bridge, I was relegated to the wardroom, which was reached from a small penthouse on deck, via an iron ladder. Out into the straits the destroyer started to girate as only a destroyer can, heave up, plunge down, yaw sideways. With difficulty I heaved myself up the ladder and sat on my suitcases above. The sliding door to the deck was a few inches ajar, and through the gap the spray poured in. Shortly there were three inches of seawater milling about the floor. Things quietened down, and a sailor entered, grabbed my cases and led me to the side of the ship. There, half a mile away, was Courageous, and half-way rowing towards us came a gig. As it came alongside the coxswain shouted:

"I have only four lifebelts, Sir."

The crew were all girded in cork lifebelts. I counted quickly; there was the Admiral, his Flag Commander, the (air) Wing Commander and a sailor. Holder was the fifth! At one moment the gig was level with the destroyer's deck. A moment later it was twelve feet down. Flags, the Airman and the sailor were got aboard while I stood aside for the Admiral, but owing to naval etiquette he was to be the last to leave. I was seized by a Petty Officer and launched into space. I landed somehow among a welter of seats and bodies without breaking a leg, the Admiral arrived, and the order was given to 'give way'.

* * *

My car arrived on Derby Day, and I collected it from the docks. I parked it on the opposite side of Piccadilly from the Cavalry Club. Looking out of my bedroom window next morning, I spied a policeman in attendance. No nonsense about meters in those days, but apparently it was not allowed to park overnight. I donned my bowler and advanced towards the Chrysler. The constable asked:

"Is this your car Sir?"

"Yes, officer, isn't she a beauty?"

"No doubt about that, Sir. But the regulations ..."

"Oh, I didn't know about that. I will take it away."
I sat in the car. The battery was flat. I appealed to the constable.

"Well, Sir, it seems that we will have to give her a push."
And summoning a taxi-driver form the rank, the two of them got me going.

During my leaves I was privileged to meet two remarkable women. The first was the fabulous Rosa Lewis, the chatelaine of the Cavendish Hotel, Jermyn Street. The Cavendish was really an inn in the centre of London. I was told it was given to Rosa by H.M. King Edward VII. Its coffee room opened on to the forecourt, a largish area of grass interspersed with a few cut shrubs and pieces of statuary. Its passages and its hall contained some very nice pieces of furniture and old sporting prints. If I came down to breakfast and there was no one about I shouted down the kitchen stairs:

"Anything to eat to-day?"
Came the answer in broad cockney,

"All right Major, what do you want?"
They produced a good breakfast. For those that Rosa accepted, the Cavendish was a very special and discreet rendezvous. It could be entered, if need be, from a back door and staircase from Smith's Yard, where one parked one's car. Rosa claimed that the parking along her back wall belonged to the hotel and woe betide Smith if he put a customer's car there. Should he do so and it came to Rosa's notice she would make a fishwife blush. The offending vehicle was instantly removed.

In the famous 'front room', to which Rosa's specials had the entree, there was a three-quarter length portrait of her as a young woman, painted by the leading artist of the day, and depicting what was held to be 'the most beautiful woman in Europe'. The portrait, somewhat marred by holes where a bottle of champagne and a glass or two had holed it, showed a young woman on the threshold of life and, for her, what a life it was. I once offered to buy the picture off her as a memento of those days, but I could not afford the price she asked. Rosa was a great one for advice to the young. She was for some reason very "anti" the Cavalry Club.

"That bloody place - what do you want to go there for? Wasting your money, drinking more than is good for you"

Young Cavalry and Guards Officers would gather at the hotel and Rosa's great expression was:

"Now we will all have a little drink."

In the front room, of course, and if there was an American around, he would be invited in and the champers would be debited to his bill. He was delighted to oblige in order to be included in that company.

After the 1939 war, Rosa was a very old lady, but always beautifully turned out in a grey silk dress with lace at her throat. She spent most of the day sitting at the desk in the hall and quite often slept over it.

Her guests thought nothing of leaving their London clothes in the wardrobes of the rooms that they had occupied. Three weeks after returning home from a stay there, I complained that I was short of two evening shirts and a white waist-coat. Laundry books were consulted, no clue. Some months later when I again occupied the same room, there in the chest of drawers were my things.

In the 50's the place went rapidly downhill, the windows and paintwork were dirty, the service negligible. But, with all the war-earned money about and pressure for accommodation, there was always room for us at the Cavendish. Dear Rosa, she had a heart of gold, and discounted many a young man's bill when he was short of funds. She had the key to Buckingham Palace garden if she wished to walk there, as did my second notable, Sister Agnes Keyser, through permission of the same monarch. It was she who dominated the King Edward VII Hospital. She was tiny and very slim and trim. When I met her, her sweet face was lined beyond belief. She had tremendous compassion for her patients, ran the hospital with a rod of iron, and no patient went under the anaesthetic without Sister Agnes holding his hand. Florence Nightingale, Nurse Cavell and Sister Agnes, they were all of the same mould.

It was becoming the thing in 1935, for those who could afford it, to fly home for their two months' leave, a matter of five days flying from Karachi to Croydon. It had the added attraction that one's leave started on the day that one landed in England. I travelled by air that year in one of the old Hannibal Class machines, a four-engined biplane with a top speed of 85

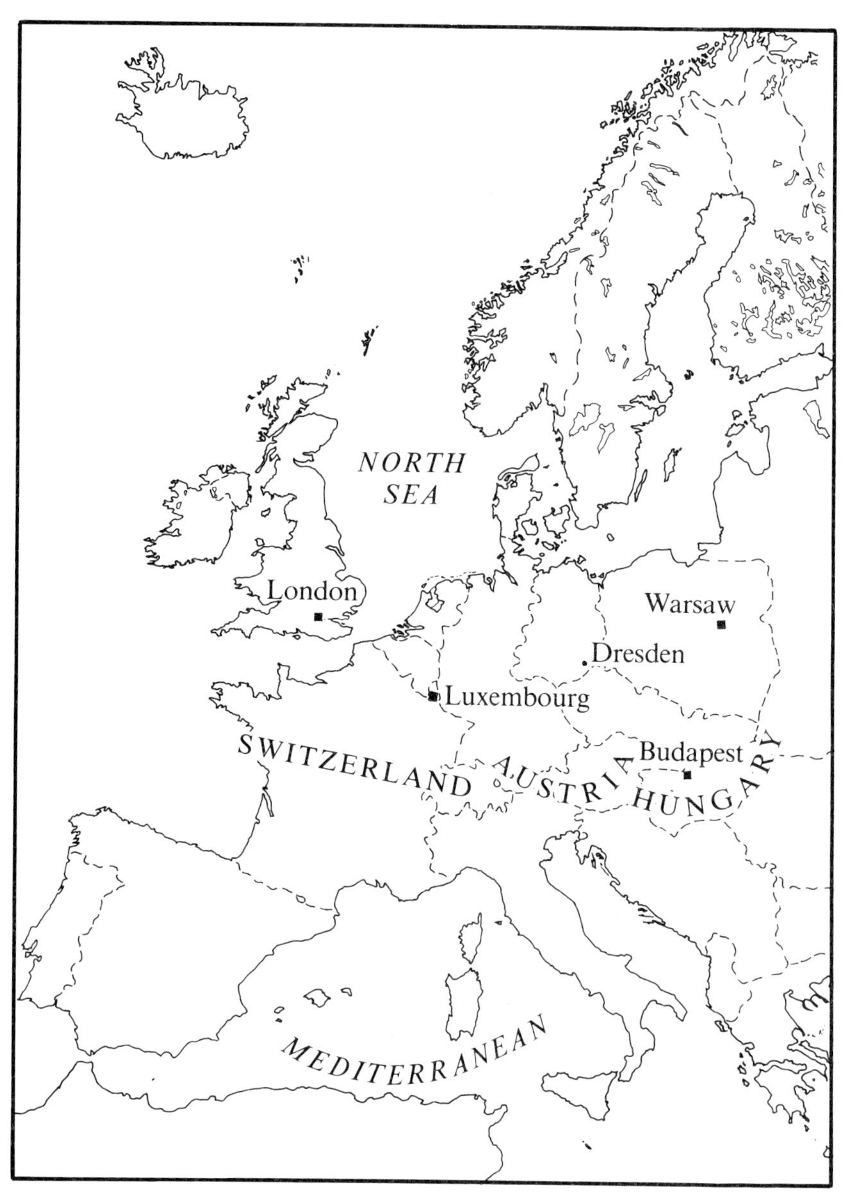

London - Dresden - London

mph. The contraption seemed to be held together with wires and, as the engines revved up for take off, the wings appeared to bend back under the strain. From Karachi we came down every 300 miles or so to re-fuel. Plugging along the Persian Gulf at a height of 200 feet one was mindful that if an engine coughed we would have dived into the shark-infested sea. But these aircraft were extremely reliable, and during all the years that they were in service, I only heard of one engine failure. Flying, in those days, was more fun because at no great height one could look down at the countryside beneath, unlike to-day, when one whizzes up to 30,000 feet and sees nothing. Five days will seem an eternity to those flying to-day when you can do it in an afternoon, but it was considerably less than the three weeks that it took by sea, or two weeks if one travelled across France by train.

I played some polo on the Beaufort Hunt grounds at Westonbirt, and there I met Angela Mackirdy. Angela was a lovely girl, I think the only woman that I have ever met who has no bitchiness in her character. We shared many interests: riding, fishing, motoring. She was a very good tennis player, and later became a very fair shot. At the end of this leave I returned to Risalpur on the North West Frontier.

In 1936 I was home again, by air, and Angela and I became engaged. The following year I had long (eight months), leave and we were married in Malmesbury Abbey - the Mackirdy family's church, on the 21st April. I call that my 'Holy week'. I was married on the 21st, born on the 22nd, 23rd is St. George's Day and on the 24th I was first commissioned. We always throw a party that week.

Angela met me at Southampton when I landed in an 'Empire Flying Boat' at the end of March 1937. Hamidulla the Rajah of Bhopal, a 9 handicap player and a friend from Bombay days, was over from India for the London polo season, and was getting his team used to English conditions at the Westonbirt grounds a few miles away. He was asked to the wedding, and my sister's children were all agog to see the Indian prince. Hamidulla arrived in a morning coat and his A.D.C. in Indian dress with a turban. My six year old niece,

Our Wedding Day, 1937.

watching intently for their entrance and, sitting just behind me and my best man, Mike Macmullen, suddenly let out a stage whisper that could be heard all over the Abbey:

"Uncle Denzil, Uncle Denzil, the black man has arrived."

Relating the incident later to the Nabob, I substituted the "The King of India has arrived"; which amused him greatly. A film was taken of the wedding and a week later it was shown at the local cinema. Bhopal's staff phoned requesting a box; the country woman in charge told us:

"I told 'im we had no boxes so I booked 'im in for three one and sixpennies."

I enjoyed the wedding enormously; lots of my friends came along, and the town altered their early closing day to see the Squire's daughter tied up. Angela's father, Captain 'Scottie' Mackirdy, had been mayor of Malmesbury, the smallest borough in England, for years, and had done much for the town in many ways. He was a great shot, and had served with the Blues in the 1914-18 war.

Harking back to 1936, when I asked for his daughter's hand, the shock to her parents was considerable, since for their daughter to marry outside the Beaufort Hunt was a calamity not to be considered, and I left the house.

My ally turned out to be Angela's grandmother, the Hon'ble Sophia Pierrepont, who lived at Cirencester, 10 miles away. When Mamma dashed over to relate the disastrous state of affairs the old lady asked:

"But Eva, what is wrong with Major Holder?"

"Mother, he does not hunt with us."

"Rubbish," said her Mum.

Scottie in the meantime had bought an Indian Army list to see if there were any other English officers in the regiment; he was somewhat comforted to find we all were. But he said to Angela,

"I suppose you will live in a *cantonment*. What is a *cantonment*?"

I think he thought it consisted of a collection of small round thatched dwellings such as one would find in the African bush.

The Hon'ble grandmother gave Angela a 12 HP Rover car. In 2,000 miles of motoring we only had one puncture. We toured through Luxembourg, Switzerland and Bavaria to Austria, where we stayed for some days with the Mayer-Melnhofs. On to Hungary, where the Wenckheims put their villa in old Buda at our disposal, together with its staff. The day after our arrival we were hailed by Pista Betlen (the President's son) who promptly arranged a polo tournament for me to play in. We were feted for a wonderful week there; parties every night.

Budapest

One enchanting evening we spent in the New York night club on the Margret Island in the middle of the Danube, champagne, brandy and a 'tear your heart out' gypsy orchestra. At 5 am our friends saw us off and having gone half a mile or so it dawned on me that we were bumping somewhat and hove to, to find a flat tyre. A moment later the Duke of Mecklenburg roared up in his 12 cylinder Sunbeam and stopped.

"A puncture? - no trouble."

He hailed a Hungarian policeman to help, cast his tail coat on to the dewy verge, and with typical Teuton efficiency changed the wheel. The wheel changed, we proceeded up and on to the bridge (one of four beautiful bridges which spanned the Danube) to find it decorated from end to end with swastika flags. A German delegation was due to visit the city that morning. A large Nazi flag hung down over the centre of the roadway. Angela had perched herself on top of our sunshine roof, and not being all that pro-German reached up and grabbed it. She held on manfully and brought down some 100 yards of bunting which trailed behind us. It was May, it was light, police whistles blew, and it looked as though we were in for trouble when we reached the far end of the bridge. I turned sharp left, and dived down into the tram tunnel. Mercifully the first tram had not yet started and we escaped.

Hungary is interesting in that there are true Hungarian villages and also Tartar villages, inhabited by those left over from the Tartar invasions in the time of Ghengis Khan and Timarlane. The Tartar descendants are Mongolian in appearance and stronger and more virile than the Hungarians. I was told that they earn a higher rate of pay. Their women still wear a knitted form of yashmak. All the houses in the villages are built at right angles to the road, which is tree lined, to give protection from the great heat of the summer. It was Angela's birthday while we were there, and I wanted to buy her a present. I bought a finely woven woollen scarf for her; white with a silver pattern which had been woven on a hand loom of the same type as the Kashmiri single bed sized scarves, which are so fine that they will pass through a signet ring.

We had meant to go on to Warsaw, but our time was limited, and we returned through Dresden and Germany. There we met miles of mechanised columns of German troops on manoeuvres. The following year, 1938, Hitler invaded Austria, and enforced the '*anschluss*', the reunion of his Reich with his native Austria. We, if not our government, had no doubts as to the future course of events, nor, I presume, did our military attaches. How many of us remember those days? The superbly powerful German army flooded into Austria; to free the 'oppressed peoples' living there. There followed the transportation of tens of thousands of Jews to their deaths, and the diminutive Prime Minister Dolfuss was forced out of a window to fall to his death on the street below. The writing was on the wall.

This was my last leave before the war.

* * * * *

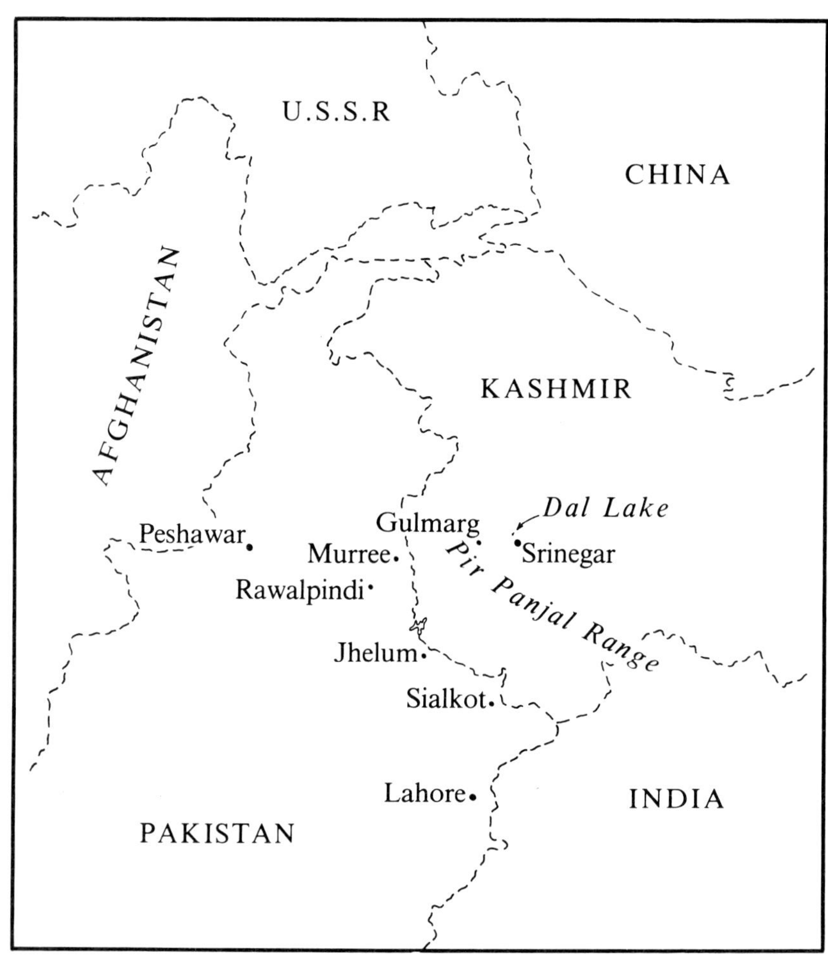
U.S.S.R
CHINA
AFGHANISTAN
KASHMIR
Dal Lake
Gulmarg
Peshawar
Murree
Srinegar
Pir Panjal Range
Rawalpindi
Jhelum
Sialkot
Lahore
INDIA
PAKISTAN

Kashmir

CHAPTER X

KASHMIR

Kashmir was an eldorado. Perhaps the most beautiful country in the world. To-day you fly there from Lahore or Delhi, but in our day you went by horse tonga and later by car, either from the south via Sialkot, or Rawalpindi from the west, in each case a journey of some 200 miles and on roads which topped 8,000ft. The Vale of Kashmir is 5,000ft and, in its centre, is Srinagar the capital - a wood-built ramshackle town, situated on each side of the Jhelum river which flows through the Punjab and joins the Indus to the sea.

When the hot weather started in Central India at the end of March, and three weeks later in the North-west, the women left for the cool of the hills. There were a dozen or more hill stations in India, most of them being on the fringe of the Himalayas, though there were others in Central and South India, and, of all these, Kashmir was the undisputed top.

In the early part of the season, April and half May, and again in September, some families put up in the main hotels or in various boarding houses in Srinagar, but the majority hired house-boats. These were very comfortable and spacious, and according to price, offered a sitting room, dining-room, and two, three or four bedrooms. The bigger boats had a large roof platform covered by an awning with tables, and deck chairs. Every boat had its accompanying cook, and servants' boat and *shikara* - a small gondola affair at the rear of which a crew of two, four or more paddlers provided the motive power. The houseboats were either tied up in berths on the Jhelum river or were poled out to any of the large lakes connected to the town and to each other by waterways. Most berths had electric cables which one could plug into for a small sum.

The boats had an outside 'running board' from bow to stern and coolies, hired for the occasion, punted the boats with long poles which they plunged in at the bows and walked along the

Dal Lake, Kashmir

boards to the stern. It was hard work and, like the captive crews of old, the coolies lightened their task with a communal song. On occasions the boats travelled at night and very romantic they looked with their lighted interiors as they crossed one of the big lakes.

Life on a houseboat was an idle and romantic dream. We bathed in water which was beautifully warm and, floating on one's back, looked at a complete circle of surrounding snow-clad mountains. It was entirely social - drinks and picnic parties, fishing for tiddlers, making love and eating the wonderful fruit - enormous cherries, peaches and apricots which were hawked round the boats by the sellers out from Srinagar, their cost being 1/10th of what they would be here.

At the European end of Srinagar was the river-side club, polo ground, golf course and tennis courts. There were the usual weekly dances in the hotel. The 'right minded' officers scorned these delights and went out shooting or fishing, travelling with a tented camp on a pony train. The fishing, all trout, was superb; there were many rivers, each divided into 'beats', and these were reserved for one or two weeks, and camp moved from one to another. The fishing licence allowed only six fish per day and, early in the day, one put back fish of less than 1½lbs hoping for bigger ones later on. Angela and I went on three such treks - one of these taking five days to reach two lakes, approximately 13,000ft high, far above the tree line, so we took all our fuel as well as our food and stores for the trip with us; chicken, flour, onions and tinned food. On these treks we took all the gear on a pony train, as many pack ponies as we needed to carry a double tent for ourselves, a cook tent and one for the staff - the cook, his assistant and dishwasher, our bearer and the pony headman; added to them was the inevitable sweeper - he who dealt with our primitive sanitary arrangements. Where the poor sweeper slept I never knew. The sweeper was the lowest member of the caste system - an untouchable, a necessary outcast. Most sweepers were good fellows and it was they who prepared the food for our dogs.

When, at the end of a long day on narrow stony tracks, we decided to camp, the outfit halted, the tents were pitched, beds set up and the cook got busy with one's evening meal. This was never less than four courses and at times we arrived in pouring

Angela and fish

rain when the ground and the fuel were soaked but within an hour, while we had a bath, the chef would provide an excellent dinner. His range was a hole in the ground under a flimsy shelter, but there he would produce, as a finale, a souffle which was out of this world. The explanation to this was that the French, who were just ahead of us in India, taught their cooks how to prepare their favourite dishes and the techniques had been passed from father to son throughout the length and breadth of India.

The Vishensar Lake which we were to fish, was at the foot of a glacier, and was frozen for some nine months of the year, but the fish were as fat as Test trout in their prime and I could never make out why! Our best fish was 4½lbs, but a few years later one of 9lbs and another of 11lbs were caught there. Today one could take an inflatable rubber boat which would give one a much better chance than fishing off the bank.

By day we wore khaki cotton shirts and trousers but, on the few occasions when the sun went behind a cloud, we hurriedly donned woollies as the temperature fell some 20°. In the evenings when the sun went down behind the glacier and its flanking 'Dolomite' peaks, we made for home. One evening Angela had a big fish on, and it had gone to ground, the sun was about to go down and I ran over and threw some stones into the water to try to shift it but without success. As the chill descended I cut the line and we sprinted for the shelter of our tent. There we sat on our beds, a rug over our knees and an oil stove under the rug, as well as putting on all the warm things we had with us; we also wore thick, thigh-length felt (*gilgit*) boots. This kept us reasonably warm. At that height the flame of our hurricane lamps did not sit on the wicks, but half-way up the lamp, and from time to time would pop and go out, presumably from lack of oxygen.

The valley leading up to the lakes contained many of the Alpine flowers which were a joy to see again, and any number of marmots - little squirrel-type animals. These delightful creatures would stand on their hind legs and whistle defiance at us and, if we went too close to them, would dive down into their holes. We passed several quite tiny lakes on our way up to Vishensar, each of which was at the foot of a little glacier. The water was a forget-me-not blue and was sprinkled with

A Kashmiri hair wash!

little white icebergs. How I wish I had had a colour camera in those days. We spent an unforgettable week there.

We returned by another route which took us down the far side of the glacier range and along the Scinde river. After walking down-stream for two days, we boarded a small house-boat to take us back to Srinagar. It was heavenly after our exertions to sit out in the prow on deck chairs and be wafted down the calm waters back to civilisation. Up in the cold we had done little in the way of bathing and, as we waited for our gear to be loaded on the boat, a couple of Kashmiri barbers appeared and offered to wash our hair. I have a priceless photograph of Angela bending over an enamel basin being attended by these two gentlemen dressed in spotless white robes. Their garb was, I may say, very different from that of the average Kashmiri, which consisted of an absolutely filthy cotton or goat-hair blanket with a hole cut for the head. They never washed and were often covered with scabies - wretched looking fellows. Their women, on the other hand, were re-nowned for their beauty and it was not unknown for one of them to accompany a 'sahib' on his shooting or fishing holiday. In Srinagar one was always being importuned by touts who hung about the club:

"Sahibs, I have lovely girl. She all right. I have many 'chits'." And they would, given the opportunity, produce a sheaf of 'chits' signed by young men who had enjoyed her company ...

The Shalimar was one of the three gardens fashioned by the Moghuls, running up the hillsides from the Dal Lake. The Moghuls invaded India from the North - I think there were five such invasions - defeated the occupying rulers and them-selves ruled the country for 600 years. It was they who built the huge forts at Delhi and Agra, various cities here and there, and their masterpiece - the Taj Mahal. Like us they summered in Kashmir and being great lovers of beauty adorned their paths with loveliness. Through the Shalimar garden they di-verted a hill stream which they led down over rock cascades into a series of rectangular pools, edged by stone paving and surrounded by trees and flower beds. These were unbelievably beautiful and peaceful. One approached by *shikara* across the lake, passing through sheets of lotus blooms - pink water lilies - floating on the surface. The loveliness of that calm water,

D.H., Srinegar

surrounded by the mountains and the gardens themselves, defies description. Small wonder then that romance often blossomed in such surroundings.

When it hotted up in Srinegar, most people moved to Gulmarg (The Flower Alp), 9,000ft up in the breast of a 14,000ft mountain, thirty miles from Srinagar, of which the last four miles had to be covered by pony, or on a litter carried by four coolies.

The motor road to the car halt, like all the roads in the Vale of Kashmir, was lined on each side with closely grown poplar trees, just as in Northern France. Terraced rice fields of the palest green, and here and there a field of bright yellow mustard, provided a lovely contrast. Ahead of the car stretched the massif of the Pir Panjal range of mountains. Everywhere in Kashmir was a delight to the eye.

At the end of the drive a mass of ponymen and coolies congregated to carry our luggage and, as we stopped, we were engulfed by the swarm,

"Sahib, you take my pony".

"Sahib, I carry your kit".

The din was deafening; there was a police Jemader to control the dog-fight and he waded in with a stick with which he laid about him, albeit with little effect. Eventually the ponies and carriers were selected and we went on our way. An hour's ride, and as we reached the top of the track, there before us was the Marg. A lovely green open bowl in the side of the mountain.

Gulmarg was the perfect holiday resort, with a polo ground, four golf courses, a hotel with 50 or more hutted quarters, and a tented camp for the bachelors. There were also numerous chalet boarding establishments for the marrieds. In the pine woods fringing the Marg were some 200 chalets that could be hired for the season, and in whose gardens grew all manner of flowers. The Marg, having no approach road, was devoid of motor cars, and everyone travelled about on '*tats*', little hill ponies, ten to twelve hands high. They were hired by the month, or, by the trip for fourpence - the owner running along in one's wake.

To play polo there, the ponies were boxed to one of the railheads, and, in charge of the orderly and their syces, plus a bullock cart for the food and gear, they marched the 200 miles, which took a fortnight. During this time the ponies became acclimatised to the height. In the 1920's polo flourished, as the Maharaja of Kashmir was very keen and the mainstay of the game, with 50 or more ponies.

Golf was the real order of the day and to play on the two main courses one had to ballot for starting times. These went from 8 am until 11.30 am and there were those who started before and after these times. It would be hard to match the surroundings of the 'Upper' course anywhere in the world. In that rarefied atmosphere one hit the ball phenomenal distances, and there was no 'rough' but numerous hazards in the form of little streams running down from the snow mountains above. At the 9th there was a club bar and, as one approached the green, a *khidmatgar* would enquire what one wanted to drink and have it ready as one holed out. During competitions a 'steadier' was very welcome.

Nedous Hotel put on a dance every Saturday night. In the 1920's these were white tie affairs, but later on it was dinner jackets and, in the war years, uniforms. After dinner the hundred or so couples, who had dined in the hotel, had to descend 140 steps from the dining room to the ball room. On more than one occasion some dear little lady would exclaim,

"Oh, Major Holder, I have stupidly left my bag upstairs".
In those days, I would go and fetch it!

Outside the ballroom was a 'pony park' where the mounts of those who had ridden to the dance waited with their attendants. On one occasion - was it Gerald Critchley? - jumped aboard his pony to find that he was also across the animal standing next door. The two ponies diverged! Why do the misfortunes of others give rise to such mirth?

Having flirted and danced in that ballroom for over 20 years it has a very affectionate place in one's memory. The same goes for the golf courses; I only played the game on those hill leaves but managed to hold on to a six handicap. In the plains it was polo, schooling and hacking one's ponies, with no time for such frivolities as golf.

From Gulmarg we fished in the Ferozepore Nullah for trout - a small river which rushed down over the rocks from the snow above. It was reached by a very steep and winding hill path which dropped 3,000ft. The Nullah held some big fish which were not always easy to come by but, on one evening, there was a tremendous take and I had four fish, all over 3lbs. Stupidly I had forgotten to bring a net and all I had to land them with was my *topee* wielded by a small boy who had attached himself to me. I cursed him roundly for those that he lost but really he was extremely skilful as the *topee* was much smaller than the fish. My ponyman carried the catch home in his blanket and we ate them, beautifully cooked, for breakfast the next morning followed by large white raspberries and cream.

On one occasion, while descending to the river, I asked the *coolie* with me if there were any snakes. The hillside was dry and sunny, a typical haunt for adders in England. The *coolie* looked to his left and said:

"No Sahib."

I asked him why he looked to the north and he replied,

"I looked to see if Haramuk" (a holy mountain to the north of the Vale) "was visible."

I asked him why and he said the gods of Haramuk deny any ground within their vision to snakes. There were no snakes!

One year I went on a ski-ing party to the snow fields at the top of the Nullah. We trekked for a day to the edge of the tree line and camped there for the night. Then we climbed for most of the next day to about 13,000ft. Being July the snow was of very poor texture but the long run down to camp was great fun if somewhat slow. Later on, when ski-ing was becoming increasingly popular in the Alps, enthusiasts started Gulmarg off as a winter ski centre. They had splendid ski-ing but of course had no hoists, and had to climb on 'skins' by the sweat of their brows to gain the height for the run down. We people had no part in this as we were tied up with polo tournaments.

The ski club built or acquired a hut at the bottom of the slopes which slept six or eight people. One night there was an avalanche which tore down the mountainside, snapping off full grown pine trees like matchsticks and completely demolishing the hut and its occupants. The damage was not so much from the build-up of snow, but from the blast of air which preceded it. Most years there are avalanche fatalities in the Alps. One year we were in St. Anton, where a party of nine were engulfed, and only four of them were dug out alive. The trouble when caught like that is that, if only buried a few feet, the skier is unable to move as his skis are clamped to his feet and he is suffocated before he can be dug out. A search is conducted by dogs, or by probing with long sticks kept for this purpose.

Kashmir offered the enthusiasts some of the best mountain shooting in the world. One rented a valley out towards central Asia and there were to be found *Markhor*, *Burrel* (large sheep), and goats, the ultimate prize being the *Ovis Amon* and the *Ovis Poli*, both of these huge sheep being as big as a pony. But to hunt these, three or four months' leave was necessary and luck at the end of it. After killing a number of stags in the Central Indian jungles from Saugor, I sickened of it. I felt an awful cad murdering a beautiful animal for personal satisfaction, and I would never do it again.

I can remember often deriding retireds. Why in heaven's name did they not go home? But I was wrong. Most of them had little money apart from their service pensions; taxation was nothing like it was at home and the cost of living infinitely less. In Kashmir they had a wonderful country and climate, all the sport that they could wish for, enough old buddies to drink with in their homes or at the club and, in the summer, hordes of their friends arrived whom they were delighted to see. On top of this they lived luxuriously in their comfortable houseboats with all the servants that they wanted. If they so wished they could afford the occasional trip home. There was much to be said for it - but, among all these pros, there is always the thought that you are not living in your own country and that niggles.

It is the same to-day for those who have settled in Spain, Portugal, Malta or the Channel Islands.

"Wonderful climate and sunshine, whisky at 60p. a bottle." But there is always that niggle. Furthermore, there is not our wireless and television. Abroad there is no Aintree, Wimbledon, Test or Rugger matches, the Derby or the Boat Race. There is plenty to be said for each side, but personally, having lived in India for 28 years, I cleave to England and its country-folk, in spite of its climate, taxation and the occasional Government I don't like. Granted I have a warm house and luckily can afford to have a gardener, shooting in the winter, and to take a couple of holidays abroad. I see great beauty in the winter countryside and, if I had to live in a cottage, I would choose to live here rather than those places in the sun. Like the rest of us I saw all too much sun in India and the deserts - when one would have given one's eye teeth for a dreary, rainy day - and I don't forget it. Nor do I want to plod about in the dust, or be very hot. Wasn't it Charles II who declared that there were more days to be spent pleasantly out of doors in England than in any other country?

Nagim Bagh, Kashmir

The Kashmiris were wonderful craftsmen and produced very fine, if rather over-intricately carved articles of furniture, mostly in finely grained walnut, the world's best papier mache, carpets, jewelry and superb embroidery on both wool and silk. All these wares were beautifully executed and extraordinarily cheap. You could buy a suit, copied from one of your own, in homespun tweed, for 7 rupees (52p.) and it would be delivered within two days of ordering. It wasn't Savile Row but those returning from service found them very acceptable.

A lot of people going to Kashmir but not particularly sportsminded, made up parties and just trekked up the valleys and across a pass into another valley. Their reward was complete relaxation, peace and the beauty of their surroundings. Alas, the life that we enjoyed so much in Kashmir is a thing of the past: prices have risen five-fold.

Above Gulmarg was the mountain Afawat, 14,000ft. To climb that height in the Alps qualifies the mountaineer for membership of the Swiss Alpine Club. In fact there was no question of 'climbing' Afawat with an ice axe, guide or ropes; one could ride up half-way and clamber up to the top with the help of an alpen-stock. The view from the summit was superb, the vale of Srinagar 9,000ft below, beyond it the snow mountains and away to the left towering far above them, the slim peak of Nanga Parbat (The Naked Goddess) 26,000ft. Has it been climbed? - I can't remember, but I know that various expeditions have met with disaster, chiefly from avalanches.

Kashmir is a Mohammedan country, while the Maharaja was a Hindu. One year up there I played for the Mohammedan Nawab of Mamdot in a match against Kashmir. The locals gathered, not too near authority, but on the slopes around the ground. Whenever we scored there were wild yells of delight from the Mohammedans. I can't remember which side won but booming away during the match was the Kashmir state band. Peter Dollar (4th Hussars), playing for Kashmir, took a swipe at the ball, sliced it and the ball went clean through the big drum. It burst, the drummer collapsed among a welter of music and stands and the band petered out amid discordant squeals and squawks.

The Nawab suffered from elephantiasis and was enormous, weighing 24 stone; his ponies staggered about under this burden and he was not, needless to say, very mobile. He had two daft 'assassins' in his team who were as wild as hawks. The 'Nabob' bellowed instructions at them from well in the rear and, on one occasion, he shouted to one of them to hit a backhander which of course he did not do. Came a wail from the Nawab:

"Ghazi, Ghazi, can't you hear the voice of your commanding officer."

He was a great sportsman and mad about his polo.

I mentioned earlier the Ferozepore Nullah and its big trout; it also held tiny snow trout. It was a popular picnic to ride down there, hire primitive rods - a withy, a cast and hook, from an individual who had cornered this sport - bait the hook with a creeper found under any stone and drop it in. At almost every cast up came a little three or four inch fish. Alongside one had a frying pan going and, as a fish was caught, it was popped in the pan and eaten a moment later - they were delicious.

Another favourite picnic was to ride up to Killanmarg, half way up Afawat, at the bottom of the present ski runs; here was a gentle slope two miles in length and a mass of flowers. In a dell, watered by a little stream running through it, I came on a ten square yard patch of edelweiss - plants people break their necks for in the Alps - and there these lovely, furry blooms grew in profusion. Alas, no gentians. Alas too, when one's leave came to an end and one headed back to the heat, sweat, dust and boredom of the plains. To catch the train from Rawalpindi, or over the 10,000ft Bannihal Pass to Sialkot, one left Gulmarg at 7 am. Riding across the empty Marg in the early morning sunlight, one reviewed the eight weeks of sport, the golf, the fishing, the last breaths of heavenly air and a last look at Afawat whose summit was wreathed in a morning mist against the bluest of skies. It wrenched one's heart. Down a hill path to the car depot and eight hours drive along the Jhelum river, up to Murree and down agan to 'Pindi, each mile getting hotter and hotter. Leave was over for that year and one faced up to reality and soldiering again, and little to look forward to until fast polo started in October. And so it was each year.

* * * * *

CHAPTER XI

CANTONMENTS

Except when on active service the Army lived in cantonments, comprising the regimental barracks of the units stationed there, their parade grounds, rifle ranges, sports grounds and the bungalows of the officers of each regiment. Cavalry, gunner, and infantry had their own areas; add to that several polo grounds and maybe a race course. A large cantonment covered several square miles. Its roads were lined with a row of trees on each side and beyond them a 'galloper' - six to eight feet of soft tan or stable litter for riding on. Beyond that a deep ditch to take away the rainwater in the monsoon. Then the bungalow compounds with their entrance drives.

Cantonments and Civil Lines were situated in less peaceful times, well apart from the native city for security and also reasons of health, since there were practically no modern sanitary arrangements in most or any Indian towns. Those stations established in the previous hundred years were laid out in rectangular form, each road or crossroad parallel to the rest, and were often named after military worthies of their time.

The bungalows stood in large compounds of an acre or so, a drive in and out to a Georgian pillared porch and, behind the house, a row of servants' quarters and a dozen stables. To the front and sides were lawns and flower beds, and the rear was devoted to lucerne beds for the horses. The bungalows had flat roofs in typical Georgian style.

The bungalow staff of a married couple comprised a bearer, the sahib's valet and personal servant who cleaned his kit, dressed him and did a certain amount of housemaiding; a *khidmatgar* (table servant) who helped in the house, a *masalchi* (washer-upper); a cook and his assistant, a nursery boy who did the Nannie's bidding, a *mali* (gardener) and his assistant, and the bullock man, whose beast hoisted the water from the compound well. Then there was a *darzi* (tailor) who sat on the

Wages - February 1938	R	A	P
Din Mahomed	41	0	0
Abdul	32	0	0
Cook & Mate	40	0	0
Ebrikim	18	0	0
Mali	15	0	0
Dhobi	13	0	0
Sweeper	14	0	0
Beasti	8	0	0
Bill Wallah	18	0	0
Richbal	116	10	0

General			
Dogs food	5	0	0
Fats etc	7	0	0
Fire & bath wood	20	0	6
Rent	90	0	0
Cook acc. Bazaar	50	0	0
Durzie	10	0	0
Small cash items	30	14	0
Small household bills	20	0	0
Butla Stores	51	13	6
Janki Peshad Stores	20	0	0
" " Petrol	14	0	0
Gov. Dairy	10	13	0
Cant. "	7	6	0
Newspapers	3	8	0
Soda water	3	0	0
15th Lanc Mess Bill	125	0	0
Jhansi Club	24	0	0
Grain	51	6	0
Imp. Delhi G. Club	13	1	0
Munchi	15	0	0

A page from Angela's account book
(1 Rupee = 1s. 4d. [approx. 6p])

bungalow verandah and did odd sewing and mending, a sweeper who dealt with our primitive sanitary (commode) arrangements and who prepared the dog food; then one probably shared a *dhobi* (washerman); added to these for one's stable was one's regimental orderly and under him a *syce* (groom) for each pony, six or seven in number. Each of these employees received very little pay - a bearer got Rs.40 (£3) a month and a sweeper Rs.12, but, together with an English Nannie, the sum of their wages was considerable and, if the servants received very little each, they only did one job; a bearer wouldn't wash up, a syce wouldn't help in the garden. Compare Western Canada, where I am told that one Chinese servant would groom, shop, cook and valet, but of course for a much higher wage. The Indian system suited India with its teeming millions, as in this way many more of them earned a living wage. Things are very different to-day, wages are much higher and cavalry officers can no longer afford to play polo as they can't afford ponies or the wages of syces.

It was the fashion in my day to deride Indian servants, comparing them to the best of English butlers, parlour and house-maids, but in fact they were very efficient and we were well served by them. The food, such as the ingredients were, was very well cooked, one's house was kept beautifully clean and I never put on underclothes, shirts, tunic or breeches which had not been ironed and produced in perfect condition to wear again.

How went a cold weather day? We were woken two hours before first parade with *chota hazri* (early morning tea) with usually a banana and a couple of biscuits; I went to my dressing-room where my bearer had hot water for shaving and washing and my clothes ready for the early morning ride. My wife had dressed and, outside the bungalow porch, were our ponies waiting to be mounted. My orderly left with the remaining ponies for exercise, and he schooled each of them in turn. On our return I changed into uniform and the *khidmatgar* brought breakfast, a glance through the daily papers and I climbed on to the horse that I was to ride on parade.

Parade consisted of occasional drill parades but more usually some sort of tactical exercise out in the country - a squadron advance guard, rear guard, recce. At the end of this we returned to the lines, where the men dismounted and unsaddled, rubbed down their mounts' backs and the troops led them to water at the long squadron troughs. The *syces* in the meantime had prepared the morning feeds and placed the feed tins at the rear of each horse standing. The horses were then picketted by head and heel ropes, hay was in the manger and the men went off to their quarters to get out of uniform and into undress for 'stables'. I rode off parade, handed my horse to its *syce* and went by car or cycle to the lines for stables. On arrival there the squadron Risaldar (senior Indian officer) met me and as we approached each troop came the order "stand to your horses", when each man stepped in front of his horse at attention, holding his animal with a hand on each side of its head collar. I walked with the Risaldar and the particular troop leaders in turn round each horse, discussing squadron affairs. At the end of the hour the massed regimental trumpeters blew the call 'water and feed' and, amidst squeals from the expectant horses, who knew the call, feeds were tipped into each separate manger. Thence to the squadron office, where there were papers to sign, programmes to be made out, defaulters (if any) to be seen and pleas to be heard. Maybe the C.O. wanted squadron commanders at a certain time, in which case I went over to the regimental office. That completed I went home to lunch.

In the meantime my wife had her ploys. In comes the bearer,

"Salaam memsahib, the cook awaits you"

Angela goes into the kitchen where each saucepan, cooking utensil etc. is presented, scoured and polished for her inspection, and she sees water on the boil for that day's consumption. Then comes the cook's *hisab* (daily bill) for his early morning marketing. The items are written in a somewhat wobbly hand and spelt phonetically ... which produced some comic results. "Item - sickins Rs.1 Annas 10."

"How come the chickens are Rs.1 10a, when last week they were Rs.1 8a?"

"Memsahib, I have served the Sirkar for 15 years and never charged one anna more than the actual cost."

In fact the cook added an anna here and an anna there and if he got away with it so much the better for him; the sum total of this villainy was only 3 annas or so a day - not a large sum!

Then there was the business of the day's menu and the issue of the necessary ingredients from the locked store cupboard.

The ingredients in our meals were not of high quality. Our meat had nothing like the tastiness of beef and mutton raised in our lush green pastures; vegetables and fruit generally matured too quickly for succulency. Bread and milk lacked quality, but our cooks were exceptional in producing excellent dishes, and what appliances had they at their disposal? No Aga or electric cooker - just a range constructed of mud which was fuelled by wood or charcoal. The dishes they prepared were put into a 'hot case' - a sheet-iron case with bar shelves constructed in the bazaar and heated by red hot charcoals to await the sahib's readiness to eat. A matter which we never fathomed was ... should we arrive home half an hour after the set time for, say dinner, and bring back three or four friends, we merely told the bearer on arrival, "So many more to supper in 15 minutes", and there was always the extra amount to eat.

Our servants ran a private system of mutual assistance. Captain "A" asks us to dine. It is a party of 8 and he does not own enough silver. As we sit down Angela spots some of our silver laid at her place. We give a dinner party and Angela asks our cook for a first-class sweet; the *khansama* (cook) tells her "Major X's cook knows a super strawberry (tinned) summer pudding - I will arrange". And Major X's cook comes over to us and prepares the dish which duly appears on our table. If Mrs. X is at the party she might think .....!

Angela (careful little Scot!) kept a monthly account book, which she still has and, as I write this, she is looking through the pages and some of the entries make amusing reading:

"Chog lad egg chers ... annas X"

This entry in fact represented chocolate eclairs.

"Cycle for cook ... Rs. 4 (30p)."

A memo that one Christmas Angela had ordered a cake, it appeared duly iced and inscribed as follows:

"Good Christmas
Good Luck
Good God"

Exercise for the day over, we had tea, played with the children, went out for, or had people in for, drinks. Another bath, change and supper.

One of the misfortunes that we suffered in India was the ravages of insects upon any material other than cotton. They would devour a picture in the course of a night, eat away a head of antlers, and wool clothing simply disappeared. In 1924 when I was Quartermaster to the regiment, my stores were cluttered with uniform cases left there by officers going on service. Their owners had been killed or had gone home and not claimed them, so it was decided to auction their contents. An auction in India always drew a crowd and we were to hold it in the Mess compound one Sunday morning. Prior to the auction I had the boxes, uniform cases and crates opened. In a so-called airtight uniform case would be a layer of white cotton drill mess kit, below this a layer of fawn dust, what had been woollen underclothes, then maybe a layer of khaki cotton drill, and below it again yellow dust interspersed with metal buttons which had been the poor fellow's Mess Kit jacket. The insects had done their work. One's bearer countered these depredations by hanging all one's thick clothes out for a few hours in the sun every week. Uniform cases were sold as being airtight and therefore insect proof, but of course they weren't. I always maintained that those serving in India should have had an 'Insect Allowance'.

* * * * *

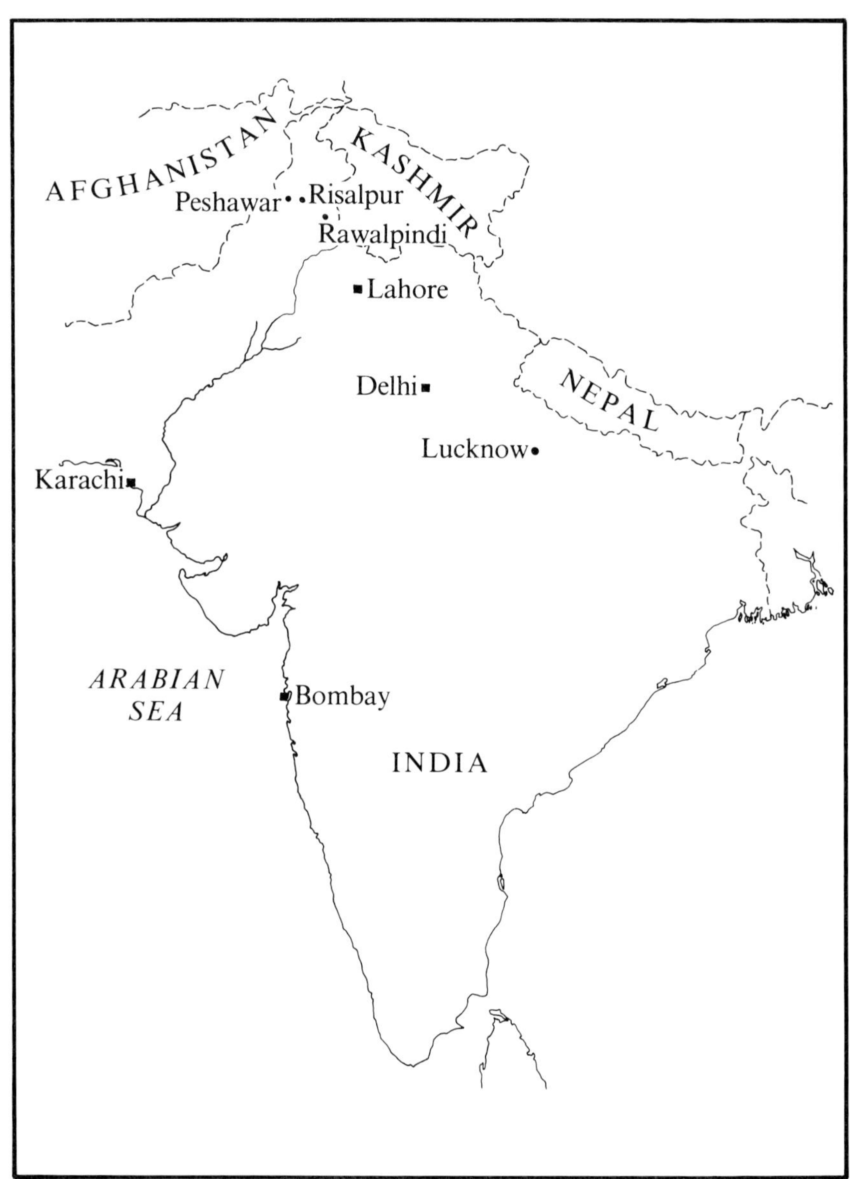

Risalpur - North West Frontier

CHAPTER XII

THE FRONTIER AGAIN

From Lucknow the Regiment moved by train to Risalpur in the N.W. Frontier Province and joined the Risalpur Cavalry Brigade - a comparatively newly built station, holding British and one Indian Cavalry regiment, a Horse Gunner Battery and a squadron of the R.A.F. The third regiment of the brigade - the Guides Cavalry - was stationed with the Guides Infantry battalion permanently at Mardan some eight miles distant.

Situated on the Frontier we had to brace up and be prepared for instant service if a neighbouring tribe started hostilities, and also have a care to the security of our weapons which were ever at risk of theft. The Pathan was a born and expert thief, and his number one objective was a British Army rifle and its ammunition. Sentries' rifles were always chained to their wrists on the Frontier. Let me illustrate.

The Guides had an American guest in their mess and, one night, this gentleman who had been well entertained by his hosts, pooh-poohed the ability of the Pathan to break in and steal. He, an American citizen, would never be caught out by that sort of nonsense. The officers in mess became rather bored as he waxed to his theme. The mess butler, who spoke English, saw that his Sahibs were being belittled by the stranger - a civilian and a type that he had the greatest contempt for. He had a word outside. The American eventually went to bed. About 3 am he awoke frozen and, stretching down for his bedclothes, found that there were none. Further exploration revealed that his bedside table, lamp and his watch had gone, as had all the furniture. All that remained was his bed, his pillow and one blanket. Then he found to his dismay that he was locked into his room, and there, perforce, he had to stay until he was called at 7 am. The butler's pals had done their stuff! How had they filched his bedclothes? Easy. The sleeper is quietly knuckled in the back and he turns over, that side of

D.H. on 'Honour Bright'
at the last mounted parade of
Skinner's Horse, Rawlapindi, October 1939.

the bedclothes is then folded over hospital-wise. Then he is knuckled on the opposite side, and the sleeper turns back. As he moves over, the bedclothes are quietly withdrawn. The operation was no doubt assisted by the victim's alcohol intake. At breakfast the American was asked if he had slept well and good humouredly he confessed to giving the Pathans best, and apologised for his boasting.

* * *

We took a team down to Rawalpindi to play in their spring tournament and in the final played The Scinde Horse. Having won all the prizes in the Imperial and Delhi Horse Show I had laid off showing, but one of our opponents, Pop Stroud, had an exceptional pony that had won the middle-weight class in various shows and finally at Delhi. I told Richball, my orderly, to watch out as to when Stroud pulled out this pony - which he did for the third chukker. I got on my star pony 'Honour Bright'. We marked each other, he being Number 3 for the Scinde Horse and I Number 2 for Skinner's. In the event I never saw him in the chukker, and we beat them 5-2. I scored all of our eleven goals in that tournament.

While we were up there the 1937 Mohmand War broke out in May. This was a biggish affair and some very tough fighting ensued. The Regiment was ordered over to Peshawar, 30 miles away, to be in reserve to the 18th Cavalry stationed there who had gone up with the column. My three seniors were on leave and I commanded Skinner's Horse. We left Risalpur at 6 a.m. and we had a hellishly hot ride in a temperature of 115^{0} or more. So I took two bites at the cherry, walking the horses to minimise the dust, and camping at 11 a.m. for that night. The Colonel 14/20 Hussars motored out and complimented us on having only two animals with saddle galls.

We were not called up to the Front but, on the day when the Peshawar Infantry Brigade were to stage the big and final attack, I took two of the squadron commanders up to a hill where we had a marvellous panoramic view of the Brigade advancing in their setpiece battle formation across the plain below us on our right, and towards the rocky heights occupied by the tribesmen. A battery of 4.5 howitzers to our left plastered the heights and in between the shell bursts we could see tribesmen dancing defiance on the topmost rocks. Then the attack went in. This ended the campaign. That day the Guides Infantry won a V.C. for the company commander who led the assault and was killed in the action, and a D.S.O. for his 2nd-in-Command, 2nd Lieutenant, Goff Hamilton. The brigade commander was Claude Auchinleck, who later commanded the Eighth Army in North Africa (1941) and was finally promoted to Field Marshal. He was always a good friend to me, especially after I was wounded in Eritrea.

Three days later there was a *durbar* (a discussion) between the Mohammedan elders and the Governor of the N.W. Frontier Province and his political officers. When the errors of their ways were pointed out to the tribesmen, no doubt fines were imposed and a cessation of annual grants declared. A *shamiana* (marquee) was pitched for the high-ups of the Army and Political Service, and two companies of British Infantry formed up on each flank to guard them. At the appointed time the tribesmen filtered in - tall, shabbily dressed, savage individuals carrying their rifles and slung about with bandoliers, many of them very handsome with fine bearded faces. Another Frontier incident was closed.

When we arrived at Peshawar, I requested, and was granted, an airplane to do a *recce* over the ground that the Regiment might be called upon to act over, and very revealing it was. Little was done in this line by the Army at that time. I had always been one for an aerial view and, with the coming of helicopters, reckoned that every brigade commander should have one at his disposal. Gradually the R.A.F. took an increasing part in frontier operations and thereby could save a lot of money and use of ground troops by (after leaflet warnings) bombing watch-towers, villages and crops of a warring tribe.

The Frontier was far from continuous action. We played polo three days a week and did a bit of shooting in favourable localities. Peshawar had a famous pack of hounds - the Peshawar Vale - and the 14/20 Hussars had a small regimental pack at Risalpur, hunted by a first-class chap, Gerald Chater, who was killed playing polo there. He was one of the five men well-known to me who met their death on the polo ground, and I suppose it was only by the grace of God that I, or any of us, were not among them. Apart from a swipe across my face, previously mentioned, I received a ball bang on the chin - the knockout blow - and another from behind on the back of my neck below my *topee*, both of which laid me out and each of which could have been fatal.

The First Lancers (Skinner's Horse) who in 1921 amalgamated with the 3rd Skinner's Horse did not in the 1914/18 War go either to France or Mesopotamia but were stationed on the Frontier. In 1919 there was another 'do' with the Mohmands and the 1st Lancers, and the 21st Lancers (British) were in on it. The tribesmen had worked their way across the border into British India in considerable force, and had hidden up in clusters of farm hutments and in innumerable patches of 8ft sugar cane. The order came through to clear them out and the C.O. of the 21st went forward with his trumpeter to *recce* a charge. As he was passing a patch of sugar cane some tribesmen emerged and shot him down. The eventual charge was successfully accomplished and this action became noteworthy in various tactical aspects.

In November of 1937 the Risalpur Cavalry Brigade were due to hold manoeuvres with the Peshawar Brigade, and our route to the confrontation would take us close to the scene of the charge that I have just mentioned. I was told to lecture the officers of our three regiments as to what exactly happened on the ground.

A fortnight previously my squadron had gone out on training, which entailed spending a night out. To be near water we had to camp close to a Pathan village. During the night and without a mosquito net I was bitten by a malarial mosquito and contracted a bad 'go' of malaria, the first since 1922, and was pretty ill with it. I recovered from the fever but was very weak, just before we were due out on the brigade exercise. Warned by the M.O., I told my Colonel that I did not think I could make it; he was tiresomely stuffy and said that he expected me to give the lecture, which I had mugged up. So, very unwillingly, I went along.

North India - the Punjab - could be extremely cold in winter, and on the N.W. Frontier bitter when the sun went down. By day the sun shone but the air was freezing. What saved us was that there was seldom a wind. If there was, we donned our *poshteen* coats like the locals who lived in them. Where the cold hit us was on manoeuvres and bivouacking out. In cantonments our horses were housed in roofed stables but with no side walls, so they were terribly chilled at night in spite of a rug and a very thick *jhool*, which was a treble thick woollen over-rug strapped at the girth and chest. The night stable guards had a pretty cold time of it also. As orderly officer I visited the horse lines at night and turned out the Quarter Guard, and I never ceased to wonder at the difference in temperature between the stifling heat of the summer and the icy cold of winter.

South India was quite different; there the climate varied little between the seasons and the houses did not even have a fireplace. They did not have the intense heat there but nor did they have our northern 'cold weather'. We plumped for the North and, mercifully, the Regiment was never sent further south than Lucknow, and thereby avoided the 'sloth belt', the stations of Bolarum and Secunderabad. The other attraction of the Punjab was the proximity to Kashmir and the polo tournaments.

* * * * *

Jhansi - North West Frontier

CHAPTER XIII

WAR APPROACHING

Angela and I left for India in October 1937. Arriving in Bombay we took the frontier mail and spent two days getting to Risalpur in the N.W.F.P. where I had to collect my car, ponies, kit etc. and my enormous bull mastiff dog, Thunder, prior to travelling to Jhansi where I was due to command our squadron in the Training regiment. During our three days or so there we were kindly put up and entertained by my fellow officers and also by the Indian Officers in the I.O.'s club. By bad luck Angela, new to the country, contracted dysentery, probably at our first meal on the train up, so the bride was not in her best shape to put a smiling face on all these festivities. The I.O.s idea of entertaining was to hand one strong whiskies and supplement these with very sticky sweets. Poor Angela. But she bravely accepted them, with, of course, further dire results. While we were there I bought her a tiny pekinese puppy. We motored down to Jhansi, in central India, some five days motoring along endless straight roads, checking frequently to avoid lines of bullock carts in the centre of the road and innumerable cows and goats led along by their owners. As I blew my horn to clear the way they scattered in every direction.

Jhansi was a very old station and the bungalows equally so. The bungalow allotted to us was a vast pile with three foot thick mud walls, the usual flat roof and a grand Georgian pillared portico. Its whitewash was peeling off; it looked dreary beyond belief. Angela took one look at it and burst into tears. We spent a week in a very indifferent hotel while our carpets and furniture were installed, and moved in.

Jhansi was a poor station, with one very indifferent polo ground. It held a British Infantry Battalion (then the Royal Fusiliers), an Indian Infantry Battalion and some Gunners. It is situated in very rocky, poorly treed country. The hot weather was hellish. The rocks absorbed the heat during the day and, when the sun went down and one expected it to cool off, the rocks gave off stored-up heat during the night, and it seemed even hotter. It had only one aspect in its favour - the shooting, duck and snipe, was first class.

A year or two previously the Indian Cavalry had been reorganised into three groups, each of six regiments, and each group had a depôt regiment whose purpose was to train their recruits and remounts. This was a sensible move, as the other regiments in the group no longer had to maintain a cadre of instructors. The three regiments chosen to take on the depot work were virtually disbanded, only retaining a C.O., Adjutant and Q.M. and the H.Q. staff, the remainder of the officers and men being drafted to other regiments in the group. These regiments were, of course, furious, but they were selected as ones who had defected in the mutiny of 1857.

Our depot was handled by the 15th Lancers. a top class regiment which had had about the best polo team in India at that time. The three 15th Lancers H.Q. staff were a very disgruntled lot, and laid themselves out to give hell to the detachments from our group. I commanded 'A' squadron, composed of Skinner's Horse and the 2nd Royal Lancers, and a pretty tough time we had of it. But I was lucky in that I had as my squadron second-in-Command a 2nd Lancer Indian who had been educated in England, and had gone through Sandhurst - Raj Kumar Shri Rajendra Singhji. He was a nephew of the famous cricketer, Ranjit Singhji. "Reggie", after we left India in 1948, become C-in-C, India. He had an extraordinarily pleasant personality and infinite tact. He was decorated with the D.S.O. in the Desert War. There were times when I blew up under our inquisition, but always Reggie stepped in with the soft explanation and put things right for me. We got through that year somehow or other, and mercifully my C.O. requested my return at the end of it, so I did not have to complete my two years' tour of duty.

Angela went home at Christmas (1938) to have our first-born, Charles. I came home on two months' leave in March, and was home when he was born, in 27 Welbeck Street. Angela's mother and I walked there along Oxford Street to the Nursing Home on Easter Monday - Bank Holiday - and there was not one vehicle to be seen along the entire length of the street.

I was recalled back to India the following month, May 1939, to attend a mechanisation course outside Poona. During our course the Major General Cavalry, Harry MacDonald, inspected the school. He spied me under a car chassis.

"Well, well, I never thought I would see Denzil Holder mending a motor car. Come here Denzil," he said.

Nettled, I just had time to get a large lump of grease into my hand, and as the General extended his hand I met it with my greasy palm. We were evens. Harry Mac, as he was known, was a splendid chap and beloved by all, and was regarded as the father of the Indian Cavalry.

One morning we were having a lecture on a complicated carburettor. There was a knock at the door and the *dak walla* (Postman) appeared:

"Cable for Major Holder Sahib."

How he knew where I was at that moment I do not know, but being an Indian he did. I opened the envelope. It was from Angela and read:

"Offered passage Stratheden 1st September - shall I take it?"

War was imminent and if I said 'yes' she could well be torpedoed, and I would never see her again. If I said 'no' I might be killed with the same result. I did not learn much about the Carter down-draught carburettor and finally replied:

"Accept passage - fearing nothing."

In fact Angela could only get a passage for herself - not for Charles and Nanny. She travelled from Wiltshire to Tilbury. Transportation was swamped with tens of thousands of children being evacuated from London to the safety of the country. Angela got aboard with the help of one of the Grindlay's directors, and then the sailing time was delayed for 1½ hours waiting for a train from the north, which never arrived. The ship was late on a falling tide and, when she did sail, it was with 90 empty berths, so Charles and Co. could have got on. Steaming down the Thames, Angela and a Guides Cavalry wife were booking seats in the dining saloon when the ship gave a crunch and listed over. It was thought that at that low tide she had struck a sand bank. The reason was not apparent until they arrived at Gibraltar, where a diver was put down to examine the ship's hull. There they found two deep scores which were obviously the scrapes of a submarine periscope which had penetrated the hull and one of the water tanks.

The Captain was in a dilemma. All shipping at that time was ordered to sail round the Cape to avoid torpedo attack in the Med. With only half his water supply, had he not taken this route, he would have to call in at various ports to replenish his water supply, and therefore be in danger of submarine attack at the approach to these ports. He requested permission to proceed through the Med, which, in the circumstances, was granted. The "Stratheden", whose economical and therefore normal speed was eleven knots, sped along with her bow in the air at twenty plus knots - and got through safely. Many of the wives had packed 'abandon ship' bags containing the barest of necessities. Angela had included a pair of stout gloves and when asked why, she replied:

"To row with, of course".

Typical of Angela. Charles and Nanny came out in January, during the 'Phoney War' period, before things started to hot up.

I rejoined the regiment in Bannu. For the first two months I could not ride as I had sprained a riding muscle in Jhansi. I had a young pony being trained to polo who was very quick tempered. One day riding her to a hot weather morning parade, she shied at nothing at all, and I gave her a quick stroke with my whip. I was feeling livery, so was she, and up she reared. Thinking that she would come down I sat tight in the saddle and gave her another one. Far from coming down she threw herself over backwards. There was then no time to hop off, and she came over on top of me - mercifully not directly - as I might have been killed, but onto my right thigh. I woke up in hospital, having been strapped against a broken rib, with Angela saying through her tears:

"You silly old man, what have you been doing to yourself?"

As I had done nothing 'to myself' I ignored her remark!

On the 3rd September we heard over a very faint and crackling wireless set that war had been declared. The regiment were ordered to Rawalpindi, and there we lost our horses and were mechanised. We left Bannu in October 1939, and within twelve months were in action in the Sudan - the second Indian

Skinner's Horse on the march from Bannu to Risalpur going through the Kohat Pass, 1938.

cavalry regiment to go overseas. If, previously, anyone had suggested that an Indian cavalry regiment could be fully mechanised in that time, he would have been written off as "barmy". We marched the 150 miles or so along the 'hard High' to Rawalpindi and arrived ten days later, spending the nights at camping grounds en route. which were maintained for this express purpose. The Army Commander came out to see us march in and, with him, Jack Evetts (now Lt. Gen. Sir John) who became a great friend of ours. Within a month our horses were drafted to other units - though we bought some of the best polo ponies. Any troop horse could be purchased for Rs.100 (£7).

Our mechanisation started with driving instruction on very ancient four-wheeled Morris lorries, and very shortly there was not an undamaged lamp-post or culvert within five miles of our lines. Later on we got more modern vehicles, and eventually were issued with Chevrolet 30 cwt. short chassis trucks, with which we went to war. Rawalpindi in the north Punjab was a big station, only eighteen miles from the Himalayan foothills, at the top of which was the hill station of Murree, (7,500 feet). "Pindi" had a high class race course alongside the cavalry lines, and just behind it was our nice bungalow.

We had a very happy nine months there - glorious weather and our last season's polo. Morning parades were at 9 am and all of us would ride out on the race course at 7.30 am in the cold but brilliant sunshine. Then a bath and change into uniform and off to parade. We had to train drivers, motor mechanics and wireless operators, the two latter categories going off on courses for this particular instruction. 'Stables' consisted of vehicle maintenance which the boys picked up very quickly. Having always cared for their horses they took an equal interest and pride in maintaining their vehicles. On service, up to the time I left, we never lost a vehicle except from shell-fire or mines. Among other things the men were told of the importance of keeping their wheel securing nuts tight. One youth in my squadron, intent on doing so, wielded his brace to such effect that he pulled the wheel bolt clean out of the wheel.

The wives left for Kashmir at the end of April, and the officers often went up to Murree for week-ends. I was there on Saturday, 17th July, when a signal arrived "Mobilisation".

That meant immediate return to duty. The following day the regiment commenced the detailed procedure to put it on a war footing. There was no snoozing in the hot afternoons, no two months' leave to Kashmir. Stores arrived from Arsenal, also our Chevrolet trucks, of which we were very proud. Then picture stencils as to how to paint on their camouflage. The colours were those of the Western Desert - a dark green and light grey, whereas when we got to the Sudan the vehicles of the Sudan Defence Force were black and dark red.

The outcrop of rock there was black and the soil very dark. Our C.O., Will Broadfoot, was posted away, and Tom Scott arrived from the 6th Lancers (which he had joined originally as a Gunner). I must say his presence greatly accelerated our training as mechanised cavalry and, in fact, his admirable training notes became a text book for future motor cavalry units. We continued to play polo and I, who had played little and rather bad polo for two years, was playing up to my old 6 handicap again, but my stamina, for some unaccountable reason, had deteriorated. Whereas two years previously I had been playing fifteen chukkers in an afternoon I now felt I had had plenty with six.

As driving instruction progressed, training drives became the order of the day, and the trucks with their high power/weight ratio had to be handled much more delicately than the old Morris lorries. Hundreds of miles were covered on the flat, and then every driver had a drive on the mountain roads. My orderly, Richbal Singh, was one of four in a truck which was descending a steepish very twisty road with a drop on the near side. The youth driving was going too fast into a right hand corner and his instructor told him sharply to brake. The driver, realising that he was heading for the edge of the drop, lost his head and, instead of treading on the brake, trod on the accelerator. The truck leapt forward and dived over the edge, falling some fifty feet. It landed upside down. One of the crew was killed, one pretty badly injured, one was O.K. but the side of the truck landed across Richbal's chest. Luckily he had fallen into a small depression in the ground so was not badly hurt, but he died suddenly three years later and, it was thought, from a blood clot sustained in this accident.

The Skinner's Horse Polo Team
Winners of our last Tournament at Rawalpindi, 1939.
L to R: George Hayes Denzil Holder Alan Dean Will Broadfoot

June was always our hottest month. After the day's work I was often too tired to get on a horse so I would take Angela out in my truck and do a bit of cross country driving. The open truck helped to cool one down a bit. Tom Scott ruled that wives were not allowed in Government vehicles, so whenever we passed his bungalow, Angela ducked down out of sight until we were safely past.

As a major, I took my turn as "Field Officer of the week". Among my other duties was that of turning out the guard on the 'Pindi Arsenal, between the hours of mid-night and dawn. We had a dinner-party and afterwards I thought - just the evening to turn out the guard. I took Angela along, I in my white mess kit, Angela in a long frock. Under a brilliant moon and sky full of stars, so bright that you could read the head-lines of a newspaper - we approached the Arsenal.

"Halt - who goes there?"

"Friend - Field Officer of the week."

"Pass friend - G U A R D T U R N O U T."

I descended from the car, inspected the guard, signed the book, patted the Guard Commander on the back for his prompt turn out and left. In "District Orders" that week appeared an order:

"Officers of the Week, when inspecting guards, will not be accompanied by ladies."

Quite right. But how had my misdemeanour reached higher authority? Maybe from a very proper Infantry Havildar of the Guard in his report. I do not think Skinner's were called upon to furnish this guard but, if we had, I cannot think that one of our 'Daffadars' would have reported the fact that one of the Sahibs had had a girl friend in tow.

After mobilisation, the Tweeds and ourselves took a bung-alow in Murree - one and a half hours up the hill - and our two wives often spent most of the week with us in 'Pindi and fed with us in the mess. We would all then spend Saturday night in the cool of Murree.

Our trucks had big balloon tyres known as sand wheels. My big Chrysler saloon was pretty well sprung but the trucks which had very stiff, light lorry springs were better sprung owing to the give in the balloon tyres.

One morning my squadron Risaldar told me,

"Sahib, there is a woman outside who wants to see you."

A woman in the office! I stared at him. He said,

"Sahib, she is the widow of a 1st Horse Risaldar who was killed in the 1919 Mohmand war, and she has a son to enlist." The woman came in, veiled, and sat on the floor. She drew her veil aside and asked:

"Sahib, do you know who I am?" I told her "Yes".

She continued, "I have a son, the only son of my husband. I have educated him in the best schools and he has an X Class certificate of education. I have brought him to serve you."

"Serve me?"

"Yes", she said. "Would you like to see him?"

He was brought in - a very comely and intelligent looking youth. We talked for a bit and I agreed to take him. The mother said,

"Sahib, I leave him in your care. You will look after him, won't you - he is all I have."

She veiled, and they went out, and we got down again to the business of the day. The boy was very well educated and I had him trained as a signaller. After I was knocked out, this boy was killed at the battle of Keren, one of the toughest battles of the war. Several months after, back in India, I received a letter from the mother.

"Sahib, do you remember in Rawalpindi that I entrusted my only son into your care, and you promised to look after him, yet you let him get killed. I now have no joy in life left to me."

I wept over that letter. All our troopers were yeomen and sons of yeomen, many of whom had served in the Regiment for sometimes five generations, ever since the regiment was raised in 1804. The eldest son joined the cavalry, the younger the infantry, and the most junior stayed at home to help on the farm. These men were not fighting for 'Democracy' or 'The British Empire' they were fighting for, in this case, us. This was the bond between our 500 men and their British Officers. You did not have to give an order - you asked a man to do something. He saluted with "*Hukum*" (it is an order). They were wonderful troops. They trusted you absolutely and you trusted them. Neither side's trust was misplaced.

* * *

It was very hot that year, but keeping going right through the afternoon, as opposed to shutting oneself away from the heat indoors, I think I kept much fitter than ever before. Maybe, also, one had an objective in life, rather than just getting through the days until one's time came for leave.

It presumably became obvious that I must do something about getting rid of my ponies. I had seven, but who then wanted polo ponies? I had two young thoroughbred mares which I sold to Probyn's Stud Farm for Rs.500 each - half the sum which I had paid for them as raw unbacked Australians. Two I gave away and the three best we kept.

About this time we found that many of the 'followers' - grooms, cooks, *dhobis*, water carriers and the like asked to leave the regiment, and their replacements were almost impossible to come by. We could not make this out. The followers, like the men, lived from father to son in the Regiment. What was going on? It transpired that the Germans had a flourishing fifth column in India which passed the word round the *bazaars* that any ship leaving India would promptly be torpedoed, and everyone knew of the submarine successes that they were having in the Channel and the Atlantic. The Indian officers were aware of this but they refrained from telling us about it lest they could be accused of spreading alarm and despondency. When we finally sailed we had a wretched collection of followers who were normally quite unemployable, but were willing to risk their lives for the pay and pension to help out their families.

September came, and we learned that we were due to leave for service overseas shortly, but no-one knew our destination. Speculation was rife: we were going to Egypt, to Persia, to Iraq, everywhere but our eventual destination - the Sudan. We were finally notified that we would entrain for Karachi on X date. Everything was packed - we marched to the railway station, some of us more sober than others. Angela and I had sat on her bed, drinking neat gin to comfort her, for an hour or so before we paraded. Some Regiment lent us their Band, and we marched station-wards more or less out of step. The cavalry regarded marching in step as a mark of inferiority - behaving like infantry - and if a young blood found himself in step with his neighbour he would promptly get out of it.

Baggage and our vehicles had been loaded the day before, so we had only to get the boys entrained. This done we lined up on the platform to say last 'good-byes', and be garlanded by those remaining behind in our depot. We officers were not wearing our breeches and boots, or even slacks, but were kitted out in infantry drill shorts with 5" turn-up buttoned to keep them in place. The idea was to let them down in thorny country to protect our flesh but the use I put mine to was to keep a map in one turn-ups, and a fid of "bromo" in the other. They served this purpose admirably.

'Garlanded'
Karachi
October 1940

The immensely long train took two days to reach Karachi, our port of embarkation. Arriving on the quay, the troopship "Devonshire" loomed above us like the Ritz Hotel. None of our soldiers had seen the sea, far less a ship. We sailed two days later, joined our convoy - a big one of fifty ships or so containing the whole of 5 Div. and its service, escorted by a couple of cruisers and two or three destroyers.

The sea was calm and we steamed slowly across the Indian Ocean. The convoy was a marvellous sight in the dappled sunshine, liners, cargo boats of every description and the light grey cruisers flying the white ensign. When we passed Aden into the Red Sea things started to happen. No torpedoes, but several times a day Italian bombers flew over and let fly their bombs, some of which hit their target. I must own that I, for one, did not enjoy the prospect of being sunk in a shark infested sea. The escort blasted off ack ack at the aircraft, which kept them well up. We were to land at Port Sudan.

Early one morning, Richbal came into my cabin and asked if I had an airmail stamp. I replied.

"Yes, thank you."

Richbal fidgeted and I asked him why he wanted the stamp. He then told me that he wanted to inform his wife that we had arrived safely. I said:

"And why the hell shouldn't we?"

His answer was:

"Sahib, ask anyone you like in India and no one would have given an anna for our chance of arrival."

This solved the business of the followers. I told Tom Scott who pitched into the Risaldar Major, who confirmed the rumours, but our men had all gone aboard without a murmur. If their Sahibs went aboard so did they also.

On the day we sailed, Angela's brother, Mike, was listening to the German propagandist - 'Lord Haw Haw' as he was known - when he declared,

"To-day the 5th Indian Division leaves Karachi in the following ships ...." (among them the "Devonshire" with D.H. aboard). "None of them will arrive at their destination which is Port Sudan."

So much for security! Rather disturbing for poor Mike - his sister a widow so early in the war!

* * * * *

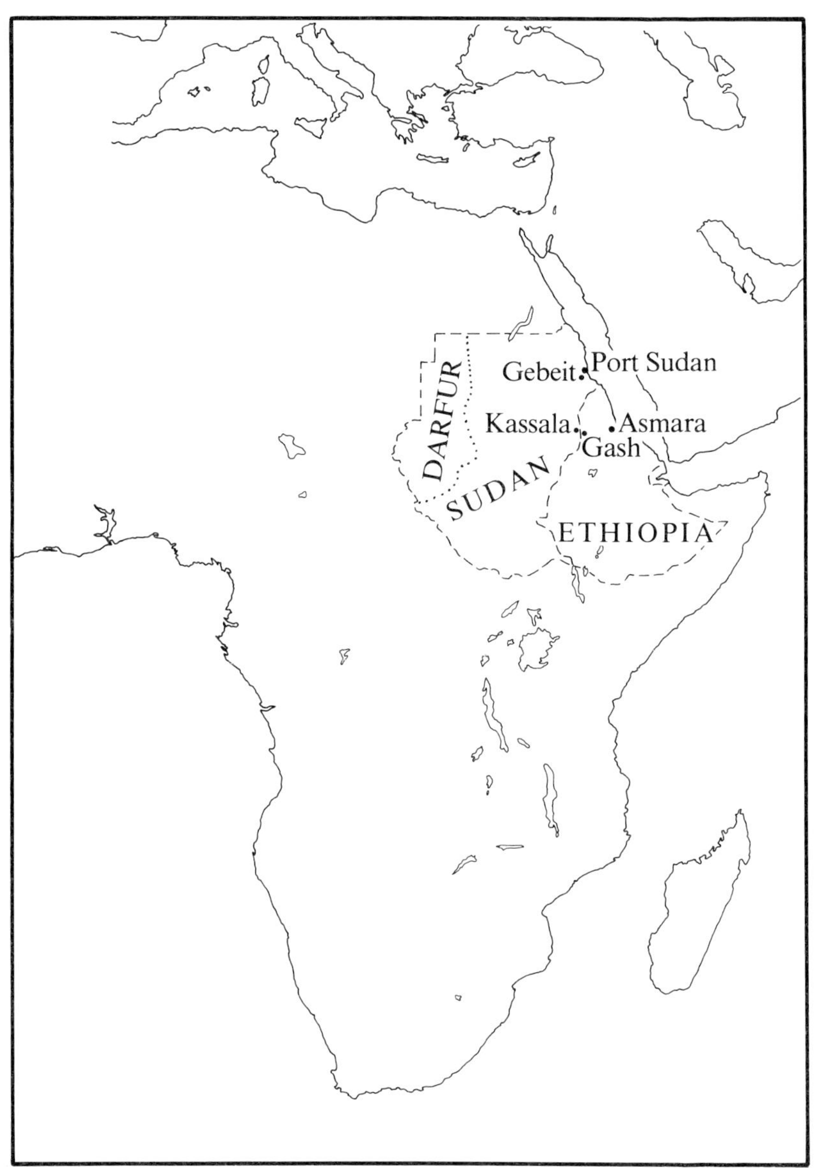

North Africa

CHAPTER XIV

THE WAR - NORTH AFRICA

We disembarked at Port Sudan and dispersed the vehicles along the shore against bombing attacks, spent three days there and left by squadrons for Gebeit, some 80 miles away in the Red Sea hills. Gebeit became our base hospital - which I was to visit twice in the next four months. Each squadron had four motorcycle dispatch riders mounted on heavy Nortons which weighed the earth; machines of a quarter the h.p. and weight would have been a lot more suitable. We encountered frequent patches of very fine soft sand in which the bikes skidded and fell over, and our light weight troopers did not have the strength to lift them up again. This occasioned continuous stops, and we eventually solved the difficulty by loading them and their riders in our trucks. Eighty miles does not seem to be much of a march, but with a few mechanical breakdowns and the motorcycle trouble we were very much behind time and arrived at Gebeit after dark. I had no idea where we were to camp, so halted the squadron and drove ahead towards lights. I was on a track which crossed over the railway line, which was built up some 8 feet above the desert. It was pitch dark - no headlights. The track rose up and a moment later we were in a nosedive over the far side of the embankment. I thought the truck would turn turtle but mercifully it landed on its front wheels and the rear ones dropped down behind us.

We joined up with the Regiment the following day and stayed put there for a week, during which time Brigadier Frank Messervy of Hodsons Horse (later Lt. General Sir Frank, and perhaps the bravest and most adventurous of our senior commanders) visited us. He explained that the Regiment, plus two motorised companies of the Sudan Defence Force (S.D.F.) were to form a column named 'Gazelle Force', to harass the Italians along the Sudan/Eritrea border. We spent the next four months doing so. The S.D.F. officers were a splendid lot; I believe that all of those employed in civil duties in the Sudan had to have won a 'blue' at Oxford or Cambridge.

Early in the War the Italians, who maintained a considerable army in Eritrea since Mussolini's 'expansion of his empire' conquest of Abyssinia, had captured the frontier town of Kassala. They probably wouldn't have done so if, by bad luck - or intelligence on their part - they had not attacked when our garrison of two companies of the S.D.F. were changing station and were caught out doing so. Having captured Kassala the Italians fortified it, wired it in, dug tank traps around the perimeter and established observation posts in the palm trees to direct the fire of several batteries of artillery on any attacking force. They had a division of troops in the area while we opposed them with approximately $1\frac{1}{2}$ regiments and no defensive box from which to operate. So, our task was not to contain them but, like the troops at Midian, to prowl and prowl around and keep an eye on things.

We moved down towards Kassala at the end of October, driving across the desert navigating by our only map - a page out of a sixpenny atlas. We knew the general direction and crossed some four or five horizons a day, often ending up by moonlight. Our marches always seemed to end under the stars, and very romantic they were; with a clear lit sky and the light colour of the desert, we got along pretty well without anything in the way of headlamps. We fetched up at Meiktila, an oasis in the Gash delta some 12 miles from Kassala, where the vehicles and tents were tucked away under the available cover. The opposition had a considerable number of tanks against which our sole defence was a 'Boyes rifle' and that was about all; it was, roughly the calibre of an elephant rifle. We had a dozen or so of these, which we posted round the camp - fearful for the worst, but hoping for the best.

The oasis was quite charming. At that time of year, there was an amazing variety of bird life - red birds, yellow birds, blue birds and innummerable Java sparrows. None of the birds showed any fear, perching a few feet above our heads, and the sparrows - somewhat like a chaffinch but with much brighter colouring - would sit on our heads, knees or the book one was reading. They were quite enchanting.

* * *

We put two squadrons out towards the Frontier, keeping the third in reserve at H.Q. The Italians had pushed out a strongly fortified post over the border into Eritrea, manned by a battalion of infantry, and it was this post that we decided to have a crack at. The post was situated on the far side of a range of hills running parallel to the frontier and we posted two squadrons on the border side of the range while I was ordered to take 'B' Squadron to the far side with the object of embarrassing communications or support from the enemy division to their outpost. We were thus cut off from the rest of the Regiment. We felt our way very carefully forward round the end of the range, which was close to the border, and positioned ourselves on one flank of the outpost, patrolling the desert around. The Italians got wind of our position and at dawn each day their bombers came over to strafe us. We busied ourselves at 5 am to get breakfast, hid our trucks in the scrub and awaited the bombing. We were more than prepared to make a cavalry charge, but not so keen to huddle in a slit trench and await the fall of the bombs. On one occasion, during a bombing attack, two of the boys in a slit trench spied a long brown snake approaching them and rather than face it they left the trench and lay out in the open. That part of Africa contained a number of snakes and innumerable scorpions - both of which were pretty deadly; the latter were often to be found at the end of a night in one's bedding into which they had crept for warmth.

It was damnably hot by day but equally cold at night. Another thing that made life unbearable was a hot dust storm which blew continually for the first six weeks, and one only opened one's mouth when it was strictly necessary. Water was a difficulty and we each only carried a canvas bag holding perhaps half a gallon of water. This, once filled, had to last us for the day or until we reached an infrequent waterhole. As one never knew when we would come upon water, having had a fill, say, at 6 am we just did not drink until the next supply was assured. There were various cases where a party having lost their way were found later with their eyes pecked out, having died of thirst. One thing was in our favour; the locals, valuing water as they did, were very careful not to get their waterholes polluted by their animals. The Sudanese were extraordinarily resistant to thirst, and I was told by one of the S.D.F. that when he was with one of their companies in Darfur, a S.W. District of the Sudan, they came upon a party of Sudanese miles out in the blue who told him they had not drunk water since the previous November. This was February. They had subsisted on camels' milk and the blood of goats they had slaughtered from time to time. They were as water-hardy as their flocks, which presumably subsisted on what dew there was.

After water, our main anxiety was the security of our command. To cover our area the three troops of a squadron were disbursed over some eight miles, while I and the squadron H.Q. took up a fairly central position. We were in wireless communication, if it worked in that hilly country, but there was little I could do to support a particular troop if they were attacked and nothing I could do if H.Q. were attacked as we had only a few rifles. I thought it unfair to one's troop leaders to pinch one of their three sections to protect us. So overnight we tucked ourselves away in the scrub and hoped we would not be overrun.

My squadron's 2nd-in-Command was a loquacious 'reserve of officers' chap who joined us after mobilisation, and he was never tired of impressing on me the tactical danger of our various positions. While we were out there he decided to grow a beard "until Kassala had fallen". A hirsute fellow, his beard grew strongly. One day I sent him off to do something or other and he ran into a party of the S.D.F. who promptly arrested him. He protested that he was British, but the soldiers argued that they had never seen a British officer with a beard, then decided he was Italian and that they would kill him. He was tied to a tree prior to his execution. Luckily for him one of their officers appeared on the scene and he was released. All this had taken time and I was very angry with him when he eventually returned, and told him that the occurrence was his own fault for being so bloody silly about his beard.

It was decided to blood the Gazelle Force in the capture of the outpost, requiring two companies of infantry and a battery of 25 pounders to carry it out. While my squadron held the outfield. In the event, owing to difficulties of ground, the attack was called off and we were ordered to re-join the

Regiment on the far side of the range. The plan was that we were to round the end of the range and retire through 'C' squadron, sent up to support us, at 9 pm, when they in turn would retire. During that day the Italians had advanced a brigade to within a thousand yards of the end of the range, presumably to relieve their outpost the following day, and there was precious little room for us to scrape between them and the hills. I put out one troop to act as flank guard under our now unbearded friend and led the remainder of the squadron round behind them. We drove as quietly as possible round the danger point and wirelessed the flank guard troop to join us, and what did he do but lose himself in the dark. There I waited for most of an hour. In the meantime 'C' Squadron had retired at their appointed time.

My squadron was in considerable danger. Would I move back leaving the 3rd troop or go on, and on waiting for them to come in? In a fever of anxiety I drank a good draught of whisky and, just as I was deciding to get the remainder of the squadron back, the 3rd Troop arrived. We sped for home. Tom Scott was in the same difficulty as I had been - whether to fall back and leave us out there or hang on as I had done. On our arrival Tom blew me up until I explained the circumstances. The Regiment arrived back at Meiktila at 2 am.

We (the detached squadron) had had a trying week. I, for one, was exhausted. We were promised a few days' rest. The following evening I had an early supper, promising myself a much needed night in bed but, just as I was going off, Tom arrived back from visiting Gazelle H.Q.

"Denzil, I want you to take 'B' Squadron out at 1 am, get in touch with the Italian outpost, and see what they're up to." This we would do from the opposite direction from which we had retired. Hell! I went to the squadron lines to plan our task. That sort of thing was the stress of war - not the danger, bullets, shellfire, bombs, unpleasant though they were, but the exhaustion, the lack of food and sleep and anxiety for one's command. I was becoming more and more exhausted as time went on. I had once been the fittest chap in the Regiment. The Italians had abandoned their post during the night and retired across the border. 'B' Squadron had just got out in time.

Everything that grew in Sudan was protected by some sort of thorn, some of them extremely poisonous. The morning after our final return to the H.Q. oasis, I trod on one of these poisonous thorns and that night my heel burnt like fire. I was in hospital for ten days after the heel had been cut open and drained.

Christmas came and went. We had been promised turkeys - a present from King Fuad of Egypt. This was to be a real occasion as our rations were deplorable except when we had shot a gazelle. The turkeys never arrived in the front line; the supply boys had seen to that. Here and there we had seen bustard, but I knew a place where I had seen them several times and two evenings before Christmas, Alan Dean and I took a truck to see if we could collect one. Alan drove very quietly in top gear and there they were, four of them. I shot one and the rest took wing. I fired again and with a fluke rifle shot I downed another one, so we had a splendid Christmas supper after all. Bustard are wonderfully good eating - far better than turkey.

When we first arrived in the desert we saw any amount of gazelle, which were as tame as the birds. We could motor past them within a few yards and they would look up and continue feeding, but after we started shooting them for food they got as shy as any other wild animal. We chased and shot them from the trucks, but later on that wasn't considered sporting and it was agreed that the driver had both to drive and shoot. This wasn't all that easy. The commoner and larger species of gazelle travelled at between 30 and 40 mph. No difficulty if one was travelling over open desert, but most of our area was thickly interspersed with scrub, trees, bushes and little *nullahs*, which the cars could not cross except at certain places. If and when we got on terms with a bunch of the quarry one had to jam the steering wheel with one's knee, take up a rifle, aim from a bumping platform and fire.

Early in January 1941, the squadron was 'investing Kassala', our forward posts being overlooked by the Italian Observation Post sentries, perched up on platforms in palm trees. They were quite easy to shoot down, but it really wasn't on to shoot a poor soldier who was only doing what he had been ordered to do, and in any case, if we did, he was only replaced by another one.

Unknown to us the C-in-C, General Wavell, moved his 4th Division down from the Western Desert to supplement our 5th Division in an advance to capture Eritrea and Abyssinia. About the 17th January, 'B' Squadron had orders to rejoin the Regiment at a given rendez-vous. Two hours before we were due to move I ordered that all three of the O.P. sentries in our area were to be shot. Horribly cold blooded, but we could not afford their prying eyes as we pulled out. On the night of the 19th January the advance started, Skinner's Horse in the Van. We by-passed Kassala and got on to the stone road leading to Asmara, the capital of Eritrea. But it was a long time, entailing some bitter battles, before that objective was reached.

It was discovered next morning that the Kassala Garrison had pulled out, leaving a token force to disguise the fact of their departure. On the evening of the 20th we were 30 miles into Eritrea, but held up by a defended village athwart the road. We hadn't slept the previous night, and had had little or nothing to eat for 24 hours. Next morning the plan was to put in an infantry attack on the village, while Skinner's were to circle round to the south, come back on to the road six miles further on, and catch the defenders as they retreated. We were in position on three low hillocks by 6.30 am but we we had been delayed by some minutes, as the terrain that we had to cross was intersected every half mile or so by steep little nullahs, many of which had to be levelled by pick and shovel to let the trucks through. 'B' Squadron was leading and if our leading truck was held up, the remainder of the Squadron spread out to find a crossing place. Being late, it became a cross country race, and eventually we arrived at our hillocks and lost no time in getting into defensive positions, one troop on each narrow ridge. We pushed patrols back towards the village, and one of them came flying back to say that enemy tanks were advancing towards us. This did not sound healthy as we had nothing to stop them with. Ahead of my hillock were 800 yards of level desert; beyond that the road disappeared into scrub trees. There was considerable mirage even at that hour in the morning; looking through my binoculars, sure enough, an armoured vehicle arrived at the edge of the open ground and tucked itself into the shade of the last trees. A second one tucked into shade on the other side of the road - but they did not seem to me to be the dark green colour of Italian armour.

Tom Scott was with me and I remarked upon this. Tom did not agree. Other vehicles arrived and fanned out to our right, and then it was clear that one was topped by a row of heads; it was an S.D.F. ("Jaunting Car") troop carrier. We were up against our own side! Shortly there were bursts of automatic fire against us. We had yellow recognition flags, and these we waved frantically, but the only response was an increased volume of fire. My right-hand troop was also under fire, and they wirelessed that they would shortly be outflanked to their right. The situation was becoming serious.

What to do?

Ronnie Coaker, the Adjutant, was with me and we decided to use our other recognition signal, that of waving our *topees*, so we crawled to the top of our ridge and waved away. A second later my arm was wrenched backwards. I had been shot in the hand. Mercifully at this juncture one of the S.D.F. officers arrived and told his men to lay off. One of the boys took charge of my hand with my First Field Dressing, poured iodine into the wound and bound it up. He was doing this when the commander of the S.D.F., "Rhino" Fosdick, arrived at our position and cried,

"Denzil, I'm terribly sorry. What can I do for you?"

Knowing that Rhino always had a few bottles of beer cooling in a canvas bucket of his highly luxurious station wagon, I said:

"What about a bottle of beer?"

"Beer", said Rhino, "Champagne is not good enough for you."

At this moment Frank Messervy arrived and yelled,

"What the hell are you fellows hanging about for? Get on."

We bolted to our vehicles.

There was a brief halt during the morning while the Italian Air Force gave us a pasting, and on we went. My driver somehow conjured up a Red Cross sling for me. An hour or so later we were held up again and someone produced a tin of sliced potatoes - an unheard of luxury. I was half way through mine when a doctor appeared and stitched up my hand, and very painful it was, rather taking the gilt off the gingerbread potatoes. Still, he did an excellent job and my wound never festered, which everything did in the desert.

We pushed on all that day and the next night and were finally stopped at a pass through some high hills, Keru Gorge, which was strongly defended. So we dug in as outposts to our own infantry behind us for the night - a most unusual role for the cavalry. We normally expected the protection of our infantry. Early next morning I got a message from our H.Q. that a Gunner Officer was on his way to site O.P.'s on my squadron front. He arrived in a cloud of dust, and we had walked together for some hundreds of yards when he took off his dark glasses and said:

"Aren't you Denzil Holder?"

He was Toc Elton, who played No.3 for the Royal Artillery Polo team. I had first met him in 1918 when he captained the R.A. Woolwich hockey team, and I the Sandhurst team. A year or two later he was shot down flying home to England.

Come noon there was a furious outburst of fire from the direction of our left rear, and bullets whistled through the bush. What was going on? Unknown to us a squadron of Italian-led native cavalry had craftily approached our left flank, unseen, along a *nullah* and, debouching from it had charged. It was a classically executed approach and their attack, pressed forward with the greatest gallantry, came in on our H.Q. A charge of cavalry can be very unnerving to troops not used to it, but to our boys it was just what we had done so often in training. The attackers were led by an officer on a white horse. Our second-in-command, Ian Hossack, grabbed a rifle from one of his men and shot the officer at close quarters. The air was thick with small percussion bombs that the attackers threw when they were within range. There was a section of 25 pounders in our H.Q. area and their gunners whipped round their gun trails and fired point blank over open sights. The enemy were also met with a fusillade from the rifles of our H.Q. and our left squadron. This was too much for the attacking Italian squadron, which wheeled away and fled.

It was thought at the time that this was the last horsed cavalry charge in history.

Meanwhile a dozen or more riderless horses galloped into my squadron area. One of them stopped a short distance from my slit trench, and started nervously to crop the dead grass. Richbal, my orderly, was nearby and I called to him to go and catch the horses. Richbal hated the war. He was not imbued with bravery, and he had no animals to exercise and school, which had been his job and interest for 15 years. A smile lit up his face and forth he went; he approached the animal, which was sweating with fear, but immediately re-gained its confidence and allowed him to take hold of the reins and mount. He cantered back to me and I said:

"How does it ride?"

His reply was

"It is very well balanced, Sahib."

I don't know what happened to the other animals when we resumed the advance.

About teatime (no tea) I took my Risaldar and Dudley Hamilton along to see how our chaps were getting on. We had reached the extreme right of our line where I was talking to two of the boys in their slit trench, when there was a sharp and violent explosion. The three of us dived into the trench, about four feet by two feet, originally dug for two men but it now had to hold five. The Risaldar beat me to it and I beat Dudley. Within moments there were five more explosions; the enemy on the hill above us were putting down four-inch mortar bombs and pretty close they were. At the fourth, Dudley let out a squeak and said he was hit; he was sprawled on top of me and I put out a hand to feel his bottom, which was above ground level, but could feel no blood. I think he had been hit by a stone. It then dawned on me that I was due to meet Tom Scott at my squadron H.Q. at 5 pm. I wriggled my left hand free and to my dismay saw it was 4.50 pm and I was 15 minutes away from our rendezvous. I had to get going. Telling the others to stay put I scrambled out and made a dash for a large tree, and from there to some scrub, where I reckoned I would be concealed. But I hadn't gone very far when there was a whisp in the air and I dived for the ground, but half way down there was a blinding flash five yards to my left. I came-to some time later, feeling rather wonky. The mortar gunner no doubt spotted my escape from the trench and with my topee and the white sling on my injured arm I was a marked man. Skilfully angling his weapon he made a marvellous shot and downed me. Subconsciously I continued onwards and came up with Tom Scott & co. He shouted:

"Denzil, where the hell ......"

and then I suppose I realised that I was covered with blood. He and Ronnie Coaker succoured me and I was put in a truck which took me back to a Field Dressing Station. I don't remember much about it, having 33 wounds from bomb and stone splinters all down my left side, including one through my left eye. I spent a miserable night on a stretcher being sick at intervals and at 4 am was put into an ambulance for the rail head - not far from our old H.Q. at Meiktila.

They had sent Richbal and my kit along with me and, but for Richbal, we might never have got back. The ambulances had come up in convoy. When the road ended, the driver knew nothing of the desert or the way back across it. Where the road met with the desert we pulled up at a tented field hospital. My stretcher was lifted on to a rack, and a doctor was attending to my wounds when there was an air raid. Thoughtfully the doctor asked me if I would like to stay there or be put into a trench, but, battered by the journey, I could not have cared less one way or the other. The ambulances whose springing was designed for European road conditions were all over the place on this rough mountain track, and if one had been a head or stomach case one would have passed out, for quite often, as carefully as the driver went, I hit the roof.

On we went across country. I was completely dopey with morphia, but at intervals Richbal shook me awake and asked me where we should head. I asked him what he could see and he would say,

"Jebel so and so is about six miles to our left front."

I would tell him,

"Drive two miles to the right of it and when we're level ask me again."

Thus and thus we got to the rail-head. Later than night I was put on to a train for Gebeit. There was no suitable food on the train, and I was very hungry. Richbal informed me that there were some *chapattis* and lentils. I opted for lentils, but only kept them down for a few minutes. The train was en

My orderly, Richbal Singh

route for Gebeit, the hospital that I had been in previously with my foot. On arrival a kind medical warrant officer seized my bloodstained corpse - I was bandaged from eye to ankle like a mummy - and carried me off towards an ambulance but half way across the platform he tripped over something, and we both crashed to the ground.

Once in the Officers' Ward I was in the good hands of Sister Kathleen Lonegan again. She was a dear. She later married our (5th) Division Commander. The two of them were later captured in Singapore, where he, poor fellow, a Lt. General, was cruelly treated by the Japs. All prisoners were ordered to salute every Jap soldier; the General had an incapacitated right arm and could not salute and for this he was unmercifully beaten unconscious.

I shared a ward with two Ordnance officers with stomach trouble, and their endless complaints were boring. Luckily they left for India shortly. My wounds were tended to, but the question of the eye remained. I asked to be flown to Bombay where there was the same Parsee Eye Specialist, but the Indian C.O. of the Hospital would not 'phone Khartoum to ask for an airlift. (The Americans would have flown me to New York in a Flying Fortress to oneself!) The eye was punctured, I knew, but I hoped it could be saved. Three or four days later the Second in Command, a Britisher, came in and told me that if I did not have the eye out I might well lose the other one. I capitulated. A young Indian doctor took the stitches out without an anaesthetic. I thought, at the end of that, nobody could hurt me any more.

* *

I was to be returned with others to India, but there was no hospital ship forthcoming. I was on my feet in ten days, and hanging about at Gebeit was tedious. Angela hated everything wrong with eyes - of dogs, or horses, and I wanted to know her reaction in my case. I need not have worried; when the casualty list appeared she learnt from a friend in A.H.Q. Delhi about me and cabled:

"Never mind darling, think of Nelson ...."

a sweet message. How I longed to be back with her, and how the days dragged. Nothing to do except walk about the rocky hillbound camp.

After five weeks or so a hospital ship arrived, and we were sent down to Port Sudan. There was the ship, white painted and red crossed, but as we queued up to go aboard there was a large notice stating "Only wounded personnel will be allowed on board". What about Richbal? He had looked after me like a child, and I couldn't bear to send him back to the conditions which he hated so much. let alone be parted from him.

The matron at Gebeit had asked me to give her *salaams* to her opposite number on the ship. I got hold of a message pad, pencilled a note to her, and told Richbal to go up a forward gangway, for the use of the crew. This had a sentry at the top and I told Richbal that if he was stopped, to say he had a message for the Matron. Once past to find his way down to the bottom of the ship, and hide there for 12 hours after we had sailed. Richbal responded with alacrity; out of the corner of my eye I saw him mount the gangway, speak to the sentry and disappear. Three days later I was looking down aft at the Other Ranks deck below, and there was Richbal dressed in complete white hospital kit looking the complete casualty if ever there was one! How he worked it and got hold of the kit I never enquired.

We disembarked at Bombay where there was a row of ambulances drawn up below on the quayside, manned by khaki-clad young women. My driver, a pretty girl, was talking to one of the other girls, and I reminded her that if we stayed on the dock-side any longer I would probably die of heat-stroke. I asked her what they had been nattering about.

"Oh", she said "the favourite for the big race."

"What race?"

"The Byculla Cup."

"What - Byculla Cup Day?"

That was the day pre-war when the Bodyguard escorted the Governor in a state drive up the race course - scarlet tunics, lances, the lot.

"Right", I said, "drive me to the race-course."

"I can't," she said.

"You can", I replied. "Straight to the course."

"You have to report to the hospital. It's my orders."

"O.K.", I said "I will report in, and then you will drive me on."

"O.K." she said.

At the race-course was the same G.H. invitation clerk, who greeted me warmly and gave me a complimentary badge. Steel Helmet, my driver's choice, won at 3 to 1. I met various friends on the Course, went to two cocktail parties and a dinner, and arrived back at the hospital at 11 pm where there was quite a rumpus going on.

"Major Holder, you were due for a Medical Board this afternoon."

Angela had been pulling strings, the outcome of which was that the Director of Medical Services, Delhi, had signalled Bombay to pass me through the hospital with the minimum of delay. The General was known as Hammy the Hun. Everybody was terrified of him and, if I wasn't through the hospital in record time, someone was going to catch it. I had my medical board (three minutes) at 8 am and was on a train in a reserved carriage by 9.30 am heading for Quetta and my darling wife.

What were my lasting thoughts on that bit of service? Best, I think, the romance and beauty of our long drives across the desert. The brilliant night skies which we learned to read for our navigating and, after a bit, cottoned on to the fact that the sky revolved ... only the North Star constellation staying put. Then there was the immensity of space and the occasional *jebels* (volcanic outcrops) rearing their heads up from the desert, like rocks out of the sea.

* *

Our troubles were, as before, those of water and the safety of one's command, and of actual fear. Fear was the thing that interested me. Most times one hadn't a care in the world, and at others one was all of a jump. Why? It was rather like waking in the morning raring to go, or feeling sluggish and out of sorts. Actually I was never scared when we were in action, maybe because I was busy; but I often was when we were hiding away, unprotected, at night. None of the training manuals touched on this aspect of warfare, but it was one of its most important features. History tells of many actions having been lost with hardly a short fired. I am grateful that I was knocked out, because I was rapidly becoming a sick man, and my nerve was going. Had I stayed on to the tremendous battles for Keren and the eventual defeat of the Italian forces, I am sure that I would have cracked, to my lifelong shame.

The other thing about War was its utter discomfort. This sounds sissy for a soldier, but, in fact, who in their senses would elect to live and sleep in the sand, always dirty and often unshaven; filthy food and often nothing to slake one's thirst. In fact, we were all too old for the ranks that we held. I was in charge of a squadron in the front line at the age of 42 whereas two years later Squadron Commanders were 25 or less, an age far better fitted to function in this role. I remember one morning in 'Pindi talking to the Squadron, who sat in a circle round me and telling them,

"Before the War is ended all of you *sowars* (troopers) will be N.C.O.s, and many of you N.C.O.s will be Indian Officers." Hands went to mouths to hide their grins.

"The Sahib is joking with us"

But of course it was true. What nice chaps they were and what excellent companions in battle.

* * * * *

Dehra Dun - North West India

CHAPTER XV

THE WAR - INDIA

My medical board had given me two months' sick leave, during which time my eye wound was to heal up and I should get myself fitted with a glass eye. This seemed simple on paper but in fact no eye is the same shape, and getting a fit is not all that easy. Bombay had plenty of glass eyes but they were invariably a somewhat bloodshot dark brown - mine being three-coloured, yellow, green etc. If I fitted in a brown eye it looked half right, half left or stared up to heaven. Further, during the previous two months, the eye socket had shrunk, and the outcome of it was that it was much simpler and less expensive to wear an eye patch - which I did, and still do.

Angela and I stayed ten days with the Evetts in Quetta, and then, in early April, left by car with our first born, Charles, his Nanny and Richbal for Kashmir. We installed Nanny and child in a very nice chalet hotel in Srinagar, and went off up the beautiful valleys to fish. The trout fishing there early in the season, like everywhere else, was at its best. We fished three beats on two rivers and had charming camps on the river banks. The quiet, the heavenly scenery and especially the green of it was balm to one's soul after the barren sand and rocks of the Sudan and Eritrea. I wasn't at all well but, in these lovely surroundings and at a height of some 6,000 feet, I was better placed than almost anywhere in the world to recover my health. The climate was ideal, with the freshness of Spring; we were together again and could not have been happier.

Two days before we were due to return the skies darkened and it started to rain. We were miles away along tracks from any made road. We did not know how long the rain would persist. If we were to get back we had to get going before the tracks became impassable. So at 7 am next morning we struck camp and went in the Chrysler back to Srinagar, leaving the pony train to follow with our gear. Coming round the shoulder of a hill, with the track sloping outwards, a rear wheel slid over the edge of the track. There was a fall of 200 feet directly down into the river and I, in the driving seat, was looking straight down into it. What to do? This was solved by a posse of *coolies* arriving who, with considerable effort and skill, lifted the car and built up the edge of the ravine until we were level again with the track. We rewarded them and pushed carefully on. The rain teemed down. Some miles further on we reached the comparative flat of a valley, but then more trouble; the track was so deep in mud that our wheels could not grip, and for every yard forward the driving wheels revolved about half a dozen times. We had to recourse to pushing, which Angela nobly undertook, and at one moment when doing so the wheels suddenly gripped and she, poor darling, fell flat on her face in the mire. It took us some six hours to cover the 30 miles to a made road. Angela was exhausted and filthy ... and it was her birthday! Still, we made it and arrived in Srinagar.

We headed for the house of a friend, Nigel Chaplin, (19th Lancers) who was attached to the Kashmir State Forces. Nigel took one look at us, shouted to his staff to produce baths, and left for the Club. When we emerged, somewhat cleaner, we found that he had secured and iced a couple of bottles of "bubbly". We had had nothing to eat since 6 am, and what with the gins, the champagne and an excellent dinner and the company, after three weeks by ourselves, we slept very soundly.

In May, when it started to get hot, we went up to Gulmarg (9,000ft) and from there I went down to India for the end of my sick leave medical board. My eye wound had not healed as it should have done, and I was given a further month's sick leave.

I was offered a Colonel's job as 2nd-in-Command of the Armoured Vehicles School at Ahmednagar. It was promotion, but again in the heat and dust of India in the hot weather, and I asked if they could find me a job in the cool of 'the hills' for a bit. I was posted as an instructor to the I.M.A. Dehra Dun - the Indian Sandhurst, in the Mussoorie foothills.

The I.M.A. was a first-class modern set-up. Lecture rooms, offices, a grand assembly hall, quarters for 400 cadets and villa bungalows for the officers and N.C.O.s. It was beautifully laid out with trees and lawns leading to a large parade ground.

Shortly after I arrived G.H.Q. announced that the place was to be extended to deal with 600 Indian cadets and a further 600 British. These latter were young men who had opted to serve in the Indian Army. A tented camp was erected for the British element and in they poured, quite often before their necessary complement of instructors had been posted. So we, at the top, were kept pretty busy organising until things had settled down. Some months later I was promoted to Lt. Colonel as Chief Instructor, and given Goff Hamilton of the Guides Infantry (now Major General) as my Staff Officer to assist in the direction of our six Company Commanders. I worked hard at re-vitalising the pre-war curriculum of training, requisite to produce a useful junior officer in the current War. I hope we had some success.

* * *

In 1942 our second son, Oliver, was born. The I.M.A. was outside municipal and cantonments limits, and therefore not under civil jurisdiction and, for this reason, we had no official birth certificate for him - which resulted in many difficulties in years to come.

I, like the rest of us, was working extremely hard. I wasn't well and many were the times when I sat down for a moment to hear the 9 pm wireless news of the War and fell asleep, and that was the end of the day's work. I contracted a nasty cough and, after two weeks of it, took to my bed.

One morning Angela came into our bedroom and there was I, black in the face on my knees, clawing at the window. What had happened was that I had coughed and, as I inhaled to get another breath, my throat shut like a clam and I could get no breath into my lungs. Angela supported and soothed me and somehow I got my breath back. I had several of these very frightening attacks. The doctors had decided to send me down to an eye specialist in Calcutta to see if I should have a new lining grafted into my eye socket. I travelled down for three days by train and saw the specialist, who advised against it, but he remarked that he did not like my cough and passed me on to an E.N.T. specialist. He told me to open my mouth and exclaimed, calling his attending students to look down my

The Indian Military Academy
1942
Headquarters Staff

throat. There they beheld a tail 1½ inches long on my uvula. This was thrashing about in my throat when I coughed, and the consequent irritation caused the spasms. He dealt with this, and ordered me two weeks' leave to be taken up in the hills, out of the heat and dust, before going up country again.

I was staying at Government House with the Herberts who kindly arranged that I should go to some friends of theirs in Kalimpong, below Darjeeling, some 7,000ft high. I boarded the train for the night journey. Travelling with me was a friend, John Burder, who was President of the Board of Trade at that time. Half an hour out of Calcutta my throat shut up again and had not John supported me I would have surely died in that carriage. Two weeks in that glorious fresh air revived me and I returned to Dehra Dun, where I had a further operation. After that I was given a month's leave, when I joined Angela in Kashmir.

My troubles corrected, and a month in Gulmarg, put me on my legs again, but another operation the following winter put me right back, and by the time I had got fit again my chances of returning to the Regiment and command were gone.

My main frustration at the I.M.A. was that, with my administrative duties, I was able to see very little of the field training of the cadets. I instituted a battalion parade each Saturday morning and inspected the cadets, along with Goff Hamilton and the Adjutant. I think I was a bit of a legend among the boys; I was a cavalryman in an Infantry establishment, I was the only officer to have seen active service, and I had a 'black eye' - my black eye patch. I kept pretty strict discipline and was regarded, I think, as a somewhat endearing tyrant. Out of the hundreds of cadets I only knew a few of the best, and a few of the worst when it was my unfortunate task to relegate or expel them. But in after years, when travelling by rail, a young subaltern often drew himself up and handed me a guardsman's salute. When I spoke to him he would say:

"You remember me, Sir, at the I.M.A.?"

"Yes", I would say, "of course I do. You were in which Company?"

"'B' Company, Sir."

"Yes", I said, "of course, 'B' Company."

They were as proud of the I.M.A., as we had been of Sandhurst.

When a company passed out as commissioned officers I gave them a farewell lecture; I told them how honoured they were to be about to lead the Indian troops in battle. How their men would size them up much more accurately than their seniors.

"You must be all asking yourselves how you will acquit yourselves under fire. You are probably apprehensive that you will be frightened, and worse still, show it."

"Now," I told them, "let us examine fear. What will you be frightened of? If you are lightly wounded it hurts like hell, but is not dangerous. If you are badly wounded it does not hurt, as nature takes care of you with what is called 'shock', and you feel little or nothing. I know - I have had both. If you are killed you know nothing about it anyhow. So what have you to worry about? Nothing!"

I hope this was some comfort to them. I remember a splendid chap, Alan Paley of the Rifle Brigade, who was Assistant Commandant when I was at Sandhurst. He delivered our final departure lecture and, mindful of the fact that in 1918 the expectation of life of a subaltern in the trenches was only some four weeks, and faced with 400 fine young men whom he had been instrumental in training for the past year, his emotions overcame him and before the end of his talk he pulled his cap over his eyes and walked off the platform in tears. He was a bit of a legend, Alan Paley; he rode a very nice chestnut horse on the parade ground and, attached to his horse's brow-band, was the 1914 Star medal ribbon. He later commanded a battalion of the Rifle Brigade in India, where none of his officers was allowed to run a motor car. They could have traps and he encouraged them to have as many polo ponies as they could afford.

I had always been a friend of that great soldier and hero of the Indian Army, Claude Auchinleck. When my time was up at the I.M.A. he was Commander-in-Chief India. He took pity on me and gave me command of a School in Pachmarhi in the highlands of Central India - the old home of the School of Musketry which every officer and many N.C.O.s had to attend during their service. Pachmarhi was not the Himalayas, but it was a plateau 4,000ft or so high, delightfully green and far distant from inspecting Generals and other troubles. We had a lovely spacious bungalow above and overlooking a large lake and there, very happily, I finished my service along with my family, added to by our third and last child, Sally. Angela had taken Charles, Oliver and our Nanny to Kashmir. In May I was in my C.O.'s office one morning and talking to my Risaldar Major Ganesh Dass Bali, when the *dak wallah* (postman) arrived and handed me a telegram. It read:

"Your daughter arrived this morning.
Both well. Best love. Angela."

We had two sons and I had hoped for, and was delighted to have, a daughter; but with true British phlegm I scanned the message and without comment passed it to the R.M. He put on his specs, read it and clasped me by the arm.

"Sahib, my utter condolences. I feel a dagger in my heart." I told him, "But Risaldar Sahib, I am delighted."

"Sahib," he replied, "you are a brave man but I shall feel for you until I die."

What he meant was that India reared many more girl children than boys and, to marry them off, the parents had to put up a substantial dowry to the proposed husband which was a disastrous strain on the family's finances. This good man, and he was indeed a good man, sorrowed for me. Nothing would have convinced him otherwise. Just before I left I was able to get him a decoration in the Birthday Honours.

Prior to my taking over the School the students were housed in barracks according to their religion, ie. quarters for Moslems and others for Hindus. I thought that the time had come to improve on this and ordered mixed barracks. The permanent staff Indian Officers were horrified but I stuck to my guns and it worked perfectly.

To the south of the Pachmarhi plateau there was a stream which, over the centuries, had eroded a chasm hundreds of feet deep. At the bottom of the chasm this stream flowed peacefully along, sometimes deep enough to swim in and at others to paddle through. It was bordered by rich ferns and other tropical looking plants - a scene of considerable beauty. On Sundays we would make up picnic parties, motor to the edge of the plateau and scramble down twisting goat tracks to the water. Our clothes, less bathing gear and gym shoes, were sent along with the lunch to one of several places downstream from which one would climb up again. Floating on one's back in the deeper waters, one looked up at a narrow patch of blue sky through the trees which grew on the sides of the canyon. Rising out of the plateau were various hills, in some of which were pre-historic caves. In one of these were brick-coloured drawings of humans and animals identical to those found in caves in the South of France.

The Central Indian jungles were renowned for their big game - tiger, leopard and stag of all sorts, also python. Pachmarhi sported one rambling hotel which had a deep verandah on which were an assortment of arm chairs and sofas. There was a leopard which regularly slept on one of the sofas. Leopards were mad about dogs and many a pet was grabbed from a bungalow at night when the french windows had been left open in the summer. We had five fox terriers and were careful to shut them up in a bathroom at night.

To the layman, India abounded in snakes but, in fact, during my 28 years there I only saw half a dozen of them. When I was doing my musketry course in "Pach" in 1930, I drove two of my friends, George Todd and Walter Loring, round the outside boundary road the evening before the course ended. In front of us crossing the road was a 7ft python. I pulled up the car and we gave chase, picking up and throwing stones at the reptile. After some 80 yards the python sought cover in a bush, but its tail was protruding by a couple of feet. Walter had armed himself with a thick branch. I told him I would pull out the snake by its tail and he would bash it with his branch. I pulled, and out came the victim and down came Walter's branch; as he lifted it up for a second whack the python was caught up in the branch, and there was Walter encompassed with snake. At that moment we fled.

* * *

In 1946 things were getting pretty tricky in India, as all the best troops were serving outside the country fighting in Europe or Burma. A lot of shirkers and the latest recruits were left in India, and these last enlisted men were of a pretty low standard. What British troops were there had only one idea and that was "I wanna go home". The Congress Party were all set to stage a rebellion in a big way, and finally to expel the British out of their country. The Authorities planned that when (not if) this took place we would go into fortified areas until relieved, or some settlement was arrived at.

As senior combatant officer in Pachmarhi I received secret instructions to plan, with the escort of our few soldiers, to transport a considerable number of wives and families, plus the students of two schools to Jubblepore, to a cantonment some 100 miles away, the transport to be civilian buses. The entire route was through jungle, at any point of which the column could be ambushed and, without doubt, wiped out. It was not a pleasant prospect. The plan was 'Top Secret' and as I could not discuss it with anyone it weighed on my mind. The operation would have been difficult enough with an armoured column and wireless communication but, with civilian drivers who would flee at the first shot, what a hope! Luckily in March of that year a Commission arrived from home, and our handing over of India to the Indians was set in train. Winston Churchill, who had been defeated in the 1945 Election, declared that we had 'scuttled' from India "the brightest jewel in the Imperial Crown" but this was not my view of the case. Had there been a nationwide rebellion it was not on for us to re-take India and no British troops after the end of the War would have stood for further soldiering in the East.

In March, 1946, Skinner's Horse returned from service, from which they had finally ended up in Klagenfurt in Austria, only a few miles from the Mayer Melnhof's house, and arrived in Lucknow. Hugh Stable, who was commanding the Lucknow district, invited Angela and me to stay with him and meet up with the Regiment. They paraded for me and I was delighted to see them again, especially my old Squadron. There they were, hardened War veterans, broad of chest and enhanced by a row of medals; they had filled out physically and I said to them:

"*Ap log* ... you people, have got fat."

To be fat in half-starved India signified both wealth and beauty. There were grins all round and the soldier in front of me said:

"Sahib, in Italy there were very good chickens",

and someone in the rear rank added:

"Sahib, *bahut acha vino bhi*" - (very good wine also).

This raised a delighted roar of laughter. Moslems are by their religion teetotallers but, away from priests and their womenfolk, they must have let up.

We were to stay on another day with Hugh but I got a signal relayed from Pachmarhi saying that we were to leave for England in four days' time, so we packed quickly. Leaving Pachmarhi, the dear old R.M. turned out the entire School - instructors and students - who lined our route and cheered us away. At the cantonment boundary the R.M. placed garlands round our necks, with tears streaming down his cheeks. How loyal they were and also how affectionate.

We travelled down to an embarkation camp outside Bombay, expecting to stay there for only three days, so we only kept a change of clothes. In fact, owing to the non-arrival of any troopship, we were pinned there for three weeks. This presented two problems - changes of clothing for the three small children and that of boredom. There was absolutely nothing to do. It was hot, and we wandered round the camp in the morning and wandered round the camp in the evening, and that was it for 20 days. The children, with no books or toys, were difficult. At last we heard that the "Stratheden" was due in the following day. What a release! We were lucky. The Stratheden was one of the most modern vessels of the P & O fleet.

Being fairly senior we had two adjoining deck cabins, and travelled in luxury. The juniors occupied flats containing 20 bunks - with one basin! Men in one, women and children in another; imagine the one basin for all your children's clothes. The ship, constructed for some 800 passengers, carried 500 children alone; they persisted in trying to climb up the deck rails. After a day of this it was agreed among the mums that if any child put more than one foot off the deck, it was to be grabbed and walloped, regardless of who owned it. Once this had sunk in, the parents had certain peace of mind. Sally was in her pram and so she was all right. Charles (seven) spent much of his time playing "Housie Housie" or "shove halfpenny" with the British soldiers, and on to Oliver (four) we tied a lable "Cabin 12". On various occasions a Master at Arms would appear with a filthy child from the bilge or engine room, and questioned "Is this yours, Mam?" Never mind, we were "homeward bound" after seven long years in India.

We sailed out of Bombay harbour on the 1st April, and there was that fine city gleaming in the sunshine, the buildings terraced up to the Parsee's palaces on the summit of Malabar hill. I thought: "In a few months the British will be out of India". We had built this city out of a mango swamp, which we acquired as part of the dowry of Catherine of Braganza when she married Charles II.

We made Southampton in 13 days, a week shorter than pre-War times. Ships, after the ravages of the German submarines, were at a premium, and the odd £1,000 of extra fuel per voyage was not then important.

We were met at Southampton by Angela's mother who had managed to obtain petrol for two cars to meet us. We were hurried through the Customs and arrived at Abbey House, Malmesbury that evening ... to a strange land of rationing, coupons and shortages of every kind. In that respect we had been lucky in India, but we gave thanks that we were at last back in the land of our birth.

Shortly after arriving home I received the following letter from the Risaldar Major :

"Most respected Sir,

With due respect and humble submission I beg to thank you very much for your kind letter of the 18th instant which I read with great interest.

Since you have left this place I am feeling very much of your good self, kind hearted Memsahib and both the Baba Sahibs. Sir, I did not feel so much when both my sons left for overseas as I feel it now when my darling Charles and Oliver separated from me. My wife and daughter are still remembering the smiling face and charming talk of our kind hearted Memsahib.

Baba Sahib's pony has been sent to Saugor. One man came to take it. Your car is being despatched to-day.

Sir, I am sorry I cannot write anything more as tears burst when I write. Please do not forget your old and obedient servant.

May God preserve you all. May God Bless you. May God protect you all from all calamaties.

Respectful salaams from self, wife and daughter to our kind hearted Memsahib and Baba Sahibs.

I am,

Sir,

Your most obedient servant,

GANESH DASS BALI
(R.M.)"

* * * * *

Back Home
Malmesbury, 1946

Charles D.H. Sally Oliver

CHAPTER XVI

LOOKING BACK

From the angle of the young man, who went out to India to earn his living soldiering, that country offered many prospects, the chief of them being sport.

The British in India were a very young lot, they arrived at nineteen and finished commanding their regiments, in the cavalry at 46 and in the infantry at 48. The higher ranks of Brigadier and Major General were each allowed a further three years service.

The Indian Civil Service, who administered the country, were relatively few in number and their work was very efficient. They were all University men who were rewarded with higher salaries and pensions in comparison with their opposite numbers in England. During my time certain measures of Indianization took place in the I.C.S., and in the Army, and this was accelerated during the Second World War.

The British have often been accused of exploiting India and this was to some extent true. On the other hand, look at the benefits that we conferred on the country - all three hundred millions of them, speaking thirty different languages. Cities were built, rail and road communications constructed, a canal service which irrigated millions of acres of parched and barren land to produce food, medical services and hospitals established, plagues and famines banished. The N.W. Frontier was subdued and the native States' rulers kept in order. Altogether a not unworthy balance sheet! The greatest benefit of all was that of peace; each man was able to live his life in safety. The country folk, 90% of the population, were, it is true, backward by modern standards, but they led secure and contented lives.

The curse of India was the love of litigation and the money-lenders. Indians would spend their last anna and more on some, to us, petty but, to them, important, lawsuit. The same applied to the cost of their marriages, when a ruinously expensive show had to be put up for which the money-lenders supplied the needful. If their crops failed the money-lenders supplied the seed for the next crop, at an extortionate rate of interest. So many, perhaps the majority, of poorer people were never out of debt. Still, the *bania* was an essential part of the scene and supplied a necessity to the lives of the poor.

What was endearing about the country people was the respect and trust in which they held us, and the *Sirkar* did not let them down. The *Sirkar* respected the religious customs of the various sects. It abolished *suttee*, the Hindu custom whereby the dead man's wives were burnt alive on his funeral pyre. This cruel custom was something that had to go. I cannot think of any other way in which their religion was interfered with.

On joining, we young officers were carefully briefed never to enter a Hindu cookhouse and to steer clear of the place where they ate their food, for if one's shadow fell on a Hindu's food it was held to be contaminated and had to be thrown away.

When polo became confined to the soldiers - mainly the cavalry - we had very few comings and goings with the civilians who, outside the big towns, were all in Government service. If we did not meet at some sport we did not meet at all. They lived in the Civil lines, the habitat of the "heaven born" - usually quite distant from our cantonments. The Army were tremendously gregarious, seldom in any week were we not out to drinks or had people come in to us. We were away and distant from our homes and relations and we clung together.

We left India 40 years ago and now they have rightly found their freedom, the ambition of all subject peoples. Good luck to them! One hears that *purdah* - the veiling of women - has largely ceased, in our day every woman wore a long head-covering scarf down to her waist, and if she met a man she would pull it over her face - a matter of modesty that she had been brought up to observe which had started in the days of the Mogul invaders, when any pretty woman was their prey. One saw the difference among the Powindas - people who travel from Central Asia into North India via the frontier passes, along with their camel trains loaded with carpets and other merchandise to be sold in the *bazaar* in Peshawar. Riding out one day in the Kurrum valley I met such a train, the men slung about with rifles and bandoliers, the women and small children, and maybe a few chickens, riding atop the camels. Slightly apart from them walked a beautiful, really beautiful, young girl. She was dressed in a mauve shirt down to her knees over pink trousers and she moved like a gazelle. As we passed she gave me a flashing smile. I have never forgotten her.

The Northern races of the Frontier and the Punjab were, by and large, very handsome. They were, and I am sure are, extremely good mannered, be they Rajah or labourer, and probably had been so when we were covered in woad and climbing about in trees.

When I first joined, all but our youngest soldiers wore beards, as did our grandfathers, but by the 30's they were clean shaven with perhaps a moustache, except the Sikhs, for whom wearing a beard was a requisite of their religion. In the 20's our men, when wearing *mufti*, wore frock coats, naturally in thin material, but again the fashion gave way to long hacking jackets.

The various enlisted classes - Sikhs, Bengalis, Rajputs, Mahrattas etc., all tied their *pugris* (turbans) in their own particular style, and one could tell a man's class and usually his occupation from the tie of his *pugri*. Every reputable individual wore a *pugri*. I dare say that this fashion has now given way to the present custom of going hatless.

I am often asked if I would like to re-visit India. Generally speaking, I think it is a mistake to return to a place where one has been very happy and I am sure, if one did so, that the result would bring disillusion. Changes there must be - as there have been in our own country.

Furthermore one would no longer be the Sahib, as of old in India but just another tourist.

What were the highlights of my time in India? First of all, of course, polo - the thunder of galloping hooves, the dash for the ball, the thrill of those few feet clearing or avoiding an opponent. Then our ponies - our capital, their performance on the ground, the price we paid for them, usually raw and unbroken, the way they were trained and what we sold them for, to buy others. I owned during my soldiering 51 ponies, and my polo cost me nothing - in fact it showed a profit. It was not just the polo games and the tournaments but the interest and time spent on schooling the ponies and riding them out

Polo at Rawalpindi
A good action photograph

non-polo day.

Then there was one's squadron, its Indian Officers, N.C.O.s and the men - admirable fellows all of them. And lastly the 100 or more horses - their feeding, grooming and their care against sickness and unsoundness. What a splendid spectacle, the squadron presented on parade! Another squadron comes to mind - that of the Bombay Bodyguard escorting the Governor up the race-courses of Bombay and Poona: lance pennons fluttering, the escort in their scarlet and gold, on truly magnificent thoroughbred horses stepping out as only a thoroughbred does - a super Ascot performance.

More thoughts ... the polo 'weeks' with their races and dances, the girls in their best frocks with their chatter and glitter. And, of course, Kashmir - the marvellous scenery.

Lastly, and perhaps best of all, one's friends. It is they who gave this Hindu Horseman his greatest happiness, through a long life, with its many memories. May I repeat that great compliment : "Denzil, I think that you have more friends than anyone I know".

* THE END *

INDEX

AUTHOR'S NOTE: This index is just an alphabetical list of names of people mentioned in the book. I apologise that their titles and rank, either past or present, maybe inadequate or non-existant.

* *indicates a photograph*